Freud and *The Da Vinci Code*
Homosexuality, Mourning and the Family in a Blockbuster Novel

Paolo Azzone

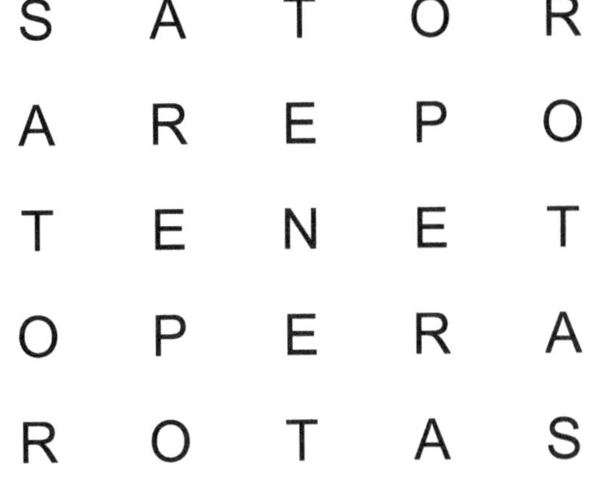

A Celestial Code

In the morning you rise,
Brilliant Phosphorus,
And your shining rays,
Around me,
Gently bend.
The birds sing.
The earth breathes.
No doubt, then:
My Grail is alive.

TABLE OF CONTENTS

On setting sail

Humans thrive on fantasies. These are necessary for our life no less than water and bread. Most of them are private or linger at the margins as family narratives. Others circulate widely, are even massively shared all over the world. Myths, religions, philosophies, political beliefs, works of art – now even corporate strategies – are able to elicit a captive interest in millions, even billion people. Apparently, interaction within institutional communities is established as well as maintained through the production and sharing of emotionally meaningful group fantasy narratives.

In our contemporary secularized society, commercial novels have largely replaced theological paraphernalia as a primary locus of socially shared fantasies. A psychoanalytic reading of one of the most successful best sellers of XXI century may so yield a valuable probe into unconscious forces which promote coalescence – though occasionally disintegration and conflict – within human groups.

Among highly pervasive and widely circulated fantasy materials the Grail mythology is all but prototypical. An old Celtic myth was shed into a chivalric romance at the end of XII century (Chrétien de Troyes, *Le Conte du Graal*) and has been able to hold an outstanding position in western literary imagery for nearly a thousand year. No more than 20 years ago, Dan Brown has breathed new life into this old narrative through his highly successful *The Da Vinci Code*.

The Grail myth revolves around an enigma. In the first known medieval version of the saga an unanswered question about the deep identity of the Grail cup yields land and cattle barrenness (Chrétien de Troyes, *Le Conte du Graal*, vv. 72-73 & 3519-3528). The very same question is an essential one to all subsequent literary adaptations, including Dan Brown's recent effort.

A basic enigma, a problem resisting any possible solution: not unlike the enigma of the Sphinx, the search for the Holy Grail amounts to a question about basic contents of human unconscious mind. In Sophocles' tragedy the core secret revolves around the violation of mother by king Oedipus. Dan Brown's late version of the ancient Grail myth is no less relevant to the goals of the psychoanalytic investigation. In fact, the reading of the novel we are here presenting will show the reader that the question of the relationship to mother lies at the core of *The Da Vinci Code* narrative, too. This time, though, beyond the veils of repression will we not unearth the mother's eroticized body, rather the mother's bones, the emotional remnants of mother's emotional degradation and death.

The Da Vinci Code has met a tepid reception among professional literary critics, and psychoanalysts were no more generous with it. Jacqueline Harpman avowed herself even unable to psychoanalytically understand its extraordinary sale success (2011, p. 35-36).

However, in writing the novel, Dan Brown proved anything but unconcerned with contemporary social and political issues. Feminist ideology and the associated political myth of an ancient Mediterranean matriarchy stand out as the ideological background against which the novel plot is skillfully weaved. A heated anticlerical polemic – a key issue in *The Da Vinci Code* – meets a no less wide consensus in contemporary both virtual and social reality. The author's ability to embed the narrative plot into issues felt as acutely sensitive by a substantial component of the expected audience played a no doubt major role in the great success the novel could gain across continents and cultures.

A deeper understanding of *The Da Vinci Code* may yield valuable information about basic beliefs which are widely shared in contemporary society. This makes it a particularly suitable object for a psychoanalytically oriented critical reading. The analysis we are reporting in the present book will show the reader that the novel manifest narrative disguises a complex, articulated, and often startling web of unconscious contents. Within this perspective an unconscious plot which will surprise the reader as directly opposing the manifest material will surface and be presented.

Over last decades, psychoanalytically oriented criticism has lost ground as a basic approach to literary texts. However, the reading of *The Da Vinci Code* we are here offering to the reader will give evidence that psychoanalysis can substantially enrich the critical understanding of a literary text. It can disclose deeper layer of meaning which stay outside the reach of conventional literary critics' tools.

Freud ushered into the psychoanalytic exploration of literary texts through a discussion of to him contemporary commercial best sellers. He believed these texts might offer a particularly productive access to socially widespread fantasies. In fact, our psychoanalytic lens proved able to unveil under of *The Da Vinci Code* manifest narrative a precious lore of information about unconscious interpersonal relationships. An underlying unconscious fantasy was revealed, featuring primal scene anxieties and homosexual strivings, manipulative interpersonal strategies and separation anxieties, splitting and projection of mother's image.

As the reader will learn from the following pages, political and ideological issues included in the manifest text could be examined and understood in a new light. Novel insights could so surface into the unconscious motives underlying powerful social trends, such as anticlerical hate, devaluation of the married couple or enhanced sensitivity to a supposedly ubiquitous patriarchal threat. From our interpretive efforts the centrality of mother's representation as a core source of well-being and emotional meaning – both at an individual and a social level –   emerged once again as a basic principle of human psychological functioning.

Psychoanalytically oriented criticism keeps being a highly productive approach to the processes of writing and reading texts. It proves able to yield information about individual and social emotional interactions and contents, which could be drawn from no alternative sources. I hope the present investigation may contribute further evidence psychoanalysis stays an essential component of the literary critical enterprise.

Part I
Psychoanalysis and Creative Writing

Chapter One
Psychoanalytical Approaches to Literary Works

The object of the psychoanalytic investigation is a human being. Generally he is directly interviewed and encountered. In supervision, however, the object of analysis, the patient, is typically absent. Humans can be the focus of psychoanalytic investigation in an even more indirect way. This is specifically the case when psychoanalytic theories and techniques (in a wider sense) are applied to the products of human creativity.

In fact, since its origin psychoanalysis has been extensively applied to myths, folklore, religion, arts, and literature. Freud genuinely psychoanalytic interest in literary texts dates back at least to the *Traumdeutung* (1900) where he named the basic unconscious constellation in both healthy and neurotic minds after the main character in a tragedy of Sophocles' (p. 267 ff.).

Of course, a literary creation is liable to psychoanalytic investigation only inasmuch as it is the product of a human being's emotional life. The unconscious continuously permeates our daily lives with concealed communications (Freud, 1901). Beside the free association flow, which the psychoanalyst elicits in the session, communicative strategies of human unconscious distort verbal communication, work schedules, technical and professional performance, and massively infiltrate human conscious fantasy activity, which obviously includes literary or artistic creation.

In fact, at a certain level, psychoanalytic interpretation of a literary text is always concerned with the writer's unconscious mental life. However, widely diverging approaches can be adopted in terms of selecting a specific focus of analysis.

The patient is present in the office, even when lending the therapist a written message or a drawing, and the alleviation of his anxieties is the object and goal of the psychoanalyst's efforts. The unconscious operations of the patient's own mind constantly control and select the emergence of the most pressing material, pushing the session focus now on transference issues, now on defence mechanisms, now on character structure, now on the reconstruction of personal history.

The scholar approaching a literary text from a psychoanalytic point of view examines the material from an as much wide array of possible vantage points. In fact, in the course of his scientific life, Sigmund Freud himself adopted a number of different approaches to the processing and use of this communicative material. We will now briefly review main strategies Freud, then his pupils and epigones, relied on in handling and interpreting creative material.

FREUD'S STRATEGIES

Wishful Fantasies

In his first systematic discussion of the issue Freud concentrated on the general emotional function which literary production and fruition can serve. In *Der Dichter und das Phantasieren* (1908a), Freud's efforts aimed at understanding the psychic forces underling literary creation, inducing the author to engage in the production of an original literary material. Freud was convinced that literary activity was basically powered by the same motivational force he repeatedly indicated as the source of dreams: the wish. Not unlike the daydream, the literary narrative would create imaginary places, times and persons through which real life frustrated wishes can find gratification.

He stated: "Unbefriedigte Wünsche sind die Triebkräfte der Phantasien, und jeder einzelne Phantasie ist eine Wünscherfüllung, eine Korrektur der unbefriedigenden Wirklichkeit" ("Unfulfilled wishes are the motivating powers of fantasies and each single fantasy is the fulfillment of a wish, a correction of the unfulfilling reality", 1908a, p. 216). He mentioned wishes of power and erotic wishes:

> Die treibenden Wünsche sind verschieden [...]. Es sind entweder ehrgeizige Wünsche, welche der Erhöhung der Persönlichkeit dienen, oder erotische. Beim jungen Weibe herrschen die erotischen Wünsche fast ausschließend, denn sein Ehrgeiz wird in der Regel vom Liebesstreben aufgezehrt; beim jungen Manne sind neben den erotischen die eigensüchtigen und ehrgeizigen Wünsche vordringlich genug (*ibidem*, p. 216-217).

> The motivating wishes are various [...]. They are either ambitious wishes which aim at increasing the standing the of the personality, or erotic ones. Among young women erotic wishes are prevailing, nearly to the exclusion of any other, as their ambition consists as a rule in love strivings; among young men beside erotic wishes the egoistic and the ambitious ones are quite prevalent.

In comparing daydreaming and literary creation, Freud noted that in daydreams the dreamer is most commonly the main agent. His wishes of social, economical or erotic success are generally represented as satisfied. On the other hand, the creative writer would display the peculiar skill to disguise the egocentric quality of his own fantasies. To this aim he creates the figure of the main character of a novel:

> An den Schöpfungen dieser Erzähler muß uns vor allem ein Zug auffällig werden; sie alle haben einen Helden, der im Mittelpunkt des Interesses steht, für den der Dichter unsere Sympathie mit allen Mitteln zu gewinnen sucht und den er wie mit einer besonderen Vorsehung zu beschützen scheint. ... Ich meine aber, an diesem verräterischen Merkmal der Unverletzlichkeit erkennt man ohne Mühe – Seine Majestät das Ich, den Helden aller Tagträume wie aller Romane (*ibidem*, pp. 219-220).

> About the creations of such writers we must first call attention to one feature; they all have a hero, who is the focus of all attention, for whom the author tries by any means to win our affection, and whom he appears to shelter by something like a special providence ... but I think that, due to this revealing peculiarity of invulnerability, you can effortlessly recognize his majesty the Ego, the hero of all daydreams no less than of any novel.

In essence, the main character of a novel would be warranted to show the most desirable qualities, to overcome the most strenuous adversities and to win the love of the most attractive woman in the novel imaginary environment, only in as far as he represents the wishes of the narrating Ego.

The interest novels are able to elicit in the general public could be understood in a parallel perspective. Through the concealment of his Ego's wishes behind the main character of the narrative – no less than "durch rein formalen, d. h. ästhetischen Lustgewinn, den er uns in der Darstellung seiner Phantasien bietet" ("through purely formal, *i.e.* aesthetic pleasures, which he offers us in the representation of his fantasies", *ibidem*, p. 223) – the writer would enable the readers to "unsere eigenen Phantasien nunmehr ohne jeden Vorwurf und ohne Schämen zu genießen" ("enjoy now our own fantasies without any reproach and without shame", *ibidem*).

Feud explicitly stated that his reflections about human literary activity referred mainly to popular literature, to novels where the exploits of a brave knight or soldier either on the battlefield or in the more gentle scenario of courting and loving the opposite sex were and are offered to the admiration of the reader (*ibidem*, p. 219). He believed the most accomplished products of literature could not be easily reconciled to the interpretative framework presented in *Der Dichter und das Phantasieren*, and suggested a more complex modelling might be needed (*ibidem*, p. 219-222).

In fact, narratives where the main character is bad or is doomed to an adverse destiny are often noted in the history of literature. They include most literary works which critics consider particularly valuable, but indeed encompass also a number of novels whose extraordinary sale success has not been accompanied by a parallel appreciation of the more sophisticated portion of literary public. The strong interest in mean narratives of unrequited love, in heroes dying due to the treason of the main bad character, and the cultural relevance and even public attraction to tragic themes in theatre plays, novels and films – consistently perceivable all through human history – clearly attest to this. No doubt: an analytic understanding of creative writing calls for a more articulated conceptualization than the one offered by Freud's first, seminal contribution to the subject.

In fact, in *Der Dichter un das Phantasieren*, Freud mentioned some hypothesis about artistically accomplished, highly elaborated, far-reaching literary works. Some other comments on the issue may be found in a posthumously published work of his, *Psychopatische Personen auf Bünen* (1905/6). In the brief paper Freud formulated the hypothesis that playwrights and theatrical audiences may share the same unconscious rather than conscious wishes.

Beside other suggestions of Freud's, we wish here to point out that he believed that aesthetic enjoyment could serve as a basic factor in eliciting the reader's attention, a function very close to that of preliminary pleasure in enticing the sexual partners to intercourse ("alle ästhetische Lust die uns der Dichter verschafft, den Charakter solcher Vorlust trägt"; "All esthetic pleasure, which the writer provides us with, serves the function of such preliminary pleasure", 1908a, p. 223). We will come back to this issue later on in the book.

The Psychoanalytic Study of Literary Characters.

In fact, in the course of his career Freud tackled literary works from multiple points of view. In *Der Dichter und das Phantasieren*, Freud showed how narratives are often powered by universal human wishful fantasies. Within this perspective psychoanalytic theory could allow the identification of main wishful fantasies included in a novel and show then possible parallel with fantasies detected in clinical work.

In *Der Wahn und die Träume in W. Jensens Gradiva* (1907), Freud approached a literary work from a radically different perspective. This time he explicitly abstained from any investigation of the writer's or the reader's fantasy life. Rather, he focused his attention on the novel characters.

Gradiva. Ein pompejanisches Phantasiestück, a novel by Wilhelm Jensen (1903), tells a romantic and puzzling story, within the speculative fictional genre. The main character, a young classic archaeologist named Norbert Hanold, falls in love with a classic age relief portrait of a young woman, loses himself in a oneiric trip to Pompei on the trail of the imaginary lover, only to meet there with an old childhood friend of his, find a real love and regain his mental balance altogether.

Freud, quite surprisingly, understood the narrative as a faithful account of a psychotic episode and its cure. He examined the main character's and his lover's psychic lives, as reported in the narrative, and applied to them the principles of psychoanalysis: "Wir Norbert Hanold und Zoe Bertgang in allen ihren seelische Äußerungen und Tätigkeit bisher behandelt haben, als waren sie wirkliche Individuen und nicht Geschöpfen eines Dichters" ("we have so far handled all of Norbert Hanold's and Zoe Bertgang's psychic productions and facts as if they were real individuals and not a poet's creations", 1907, p. 2). For instance, Freud finds in the archaeologist's longing for a lifeless engraved girl evidence of a repressed erotic wish for the dear childhood playmate. Jensen reports three fictitious dreams as experienced by the novel main character: Freud (1907, p.67 ff.) goes as far as to interpret them according to the principles of his *Traumdeutung*.

In essence, in Freud's study on *Gradiva*, literary characters are altogether equated with real life individuals and their unconscious metal life is the object of psychoanalytic interpretation. Through Gradiva, Freud introduces a novel psychoanalytric approach to creative writing, definitely independent from the exploration of daydream and waking narratives

MULTIPLE FOCI AND LEVELS OF ANALYSIS

Freud's example and suggestions for the psychoanalytic study of creative writing elicited intense research in the field since the first decade of last century. Psychoanalytically oriented clinicians developed further Freud's approaches to literature and experimented with new ones. A highly articulated investigational scenario was so brought to life.

In 1981, Meredith Anne Skura tried to formulate and classify the several approaches adopted by literary critics relying on psychoanalytic theory within a comprehensive theoretical framework. She identified 4 basic perspectives: a) *literature as case history, i.e.,* the psychoanalytic study of a literary character. Freud's essay on Jensen's *Gradiva* is a typical instance; b) *literature as a fantasy*, as a conscious or unconscious narrative, following Freud's suggestions in *Der Dichter und das Phantasieren*; c) *literature as a dream*: Skura alluded here to a perspective very close to the previous one, but with a specific focus on defensive mechanism and distorsive processes in the genesis of the literary text;

d) *literature as transference*, a sui generis projective stimulus, able to elicit typical fantasies and wishes in the readers. As a last higher order investigational approach *literature as psychoanalytic process – i.e*, as a medium adequate to activate or represent change processes – was finally added.

Skura's system is useful to our discussion inasmuch as it allows us to describe more clearly the historical changes through which the psychoanalytical study of creative writing has gone through over the last century. However, in order to formulate more clearly the issue we must understand that Skura's approach integrates two independent classification criteria.

In fact, the psychoanalytic reading of literary works has evolved through the decades with respect to two dimensions: a) *the object of investigation* and, b) *the component of unconscious life* specifically addressed. With the term object we refer here to the specific human object the critical investigation is focused on: a literary character, the author of the novel or narrative, or the reader of the literary work.

On the other hand, independently by the real or imaginary object of the psychoanalytically oriented reading, there is the question of the specific dimension or facet of the unconscious mind which is actually explored: wishes, defences, developmental fixations, Oedipal organization, quality of inner object relationships and parental imagos, personality structures, unconscious narratives, *i.e*, unconscious fantasy, epigenetic material, and so on. A psychoanalytic study of a literary text may explore either the reader or the writer from any of the mentioned specifically psychoanalytic points of view.

In the following sections we will briefly review the multiple options available to the psychoanalytic critic. We will then introduce the reader to the specific strategies we have adopted in the present book in order to decode the unconscious content of a widely known literary work.

Specific Dimensions of Unconscious Mind

I am here referring to the specific layer or facet of mental life which the psychoanalytic reader is attentive to within the emotional and interpersonal world created and represented in a literary work. Psychoanalytic models of the mind have illuminated the multilayered nature of the human mind. Freud's structural model implied a subject's manifest personality could be conceptualized as the resultant of the interaction of three psychic instances: the Ego, the Id and the Super-ego. Psychoanalysis has proved able to observe and report how such different and conflicting systems of motivation and working through of emotional experience are concurrently at work in the human mind.

The Kleinian school of thought discovered how, even in the healthy adult mind, different organizational systems including specific object relations, anxieties and defensive devices can be identified as simultaneously or consecutively in action. Melanie Klein termed such systems depressive and schizo-paranoid positions.

Wilfred Ruprecht Bion (1957), further developing Klein's ideas, has highlighted the existence within most or all personalities of a partially independent component which reflects typical wishes, anxieties, defence mechanisms, modes of thinking, and internal object relations frequently observed in patients experiencing a psychotic breakdown. He termed such intrapsychic organization the psychotic part of the personality.

An interpersonal event occurring in the relation to an external object elicits always concurrent responses from multiple components of personality. An unexpected separation from a love object may yield moderate sadness in the mature layers of personality but scare to death the primitive components of personality, reactivating the early traumatic experience of the unavailability of or separation from mother. A healthy adult may manage and control through intellectualization his love life related helplessness feelings but be met by horrible nightmares at night or gain several kilograms through regressive overeating.

In essence, unconscious communication always implies multiple layers of language and meaning. Freud introduced the principle of overdetermination (1900, p. 289) to the aim of giving adequate account of this very phenomenon. Humans experience emotional events in multifaceted ways. Within the personality different styles of emotion and information processing are always concurrently operating.

Human mind is multifaceted, multilayered. And so are the products of human fantasy life, including neurotic symptoms, parapraxes, playful activities, works of art, and obviously literary creative texts. As much varied have been the focuses of psychoanalytic approaches to literature.

Oedipal organization has been the specific object of the classic studies by Freud and his pupils (Freud 1907; Jones, 1923) on literary characters, no less than the recent reading of *The Lord of the Rings* by Jackson (2014, pp. 77-80). In Greenacre's (1955) analysis of the *Gulliver's Travels*, sexual identity is a main focus. In *The Dynamic of Literary Response* (1986), Norman Holland includes a thorough discussion of both defense mechanisms and unconsicous fantasies as detected in literary texts. He even proposes a systematic classification of fantasies associated with common literary genres or topoi. Hanna Segal (1984) has read a number of Conrad's sailor's short novels within a Kleinian framework. In her view, the main character's inhibition and general dismay with life, a quality common to all of such texts, would reflect mid-life anxieties associated with the working through of the depressive position.

The list could be lengthened at will. For the purposes of the present discussion it is important to be aware that the nature of a literary work is highly articulated. We must assume that, in most instances, anxieties, wishes and defences, reflecting most or all personality layers, find their expression in some aspect of a literary creation. Selection of a specific layer within this multiform creative reality implies an unavoidably personal choice by the psychoanalytic reader. We will not withdraw from such responsibility. We will report below the specific strategies we will adopt in approaching the text we selected for analysis: Dan Brown's *The Da Vinci Code*.

The Individual Mind
Explored by the Psychoanalytically Oriented Literary Critic

The Character

In the first half of the century, psychoanalytically informed students of literary text focused their attention mainly on literary characters. This is the approach Skura classed as *literature as clinical case*, the case being here fictitional, the case of a character, not a patient. Freud's (1907) essay on Jensen's *Gradiva* is the classic prototype. Many examples might be added. We will mention Ernest Jones' study on *Hamlet* (1923), Lacan's (1966) seminar on Poe's *The purloined letter* and Geoffrey Hartman's (1975) interpretation of *The Rime of the Ancient Mariner*.

The clinical case approach has more recently being the object of severe criticism. "Generations of psychoanalysts treated literary characters as patients seeking treatment and analyzed their pathology and dynamics. ... They neglected the study of literary traditions and genres. ... they risked missing the irony and subtlety of texts ... the complex interplay of writer and reader. This experiment demonstrates, in my eyes, the futility of reductionist approaches that bypass basic literary understanding" (Berman, 1993, p. 2). In a similar vein, Norman Holland mistrusted "diagnoses of characters as though they had walked out of the pages of fiction into a psychiatric clinic" (1975, p. 164). Leonard Jackson (2014, p. 73) wrote:

> The point is, that only in certain art forms – late Shakespearean plays, serious novels, etc. – are characters designed to have a complex internal psychological structure. Quite often, characters have a purely representative function, and no interiority at all.

Literary characters are obviously no real people. The author can admittedly try to sketch them with a view to real people he has actually met over the course of his life; however, inasmuch as they belong to the author's fantasy life, they unavoidably tend to acquire the features of the characters of human fantasies. They may appear true and convincing only if they are embedded in the writer's inner world. They possess the quality of internal, not external objects.

In fact, literary characters represent conglomerates of emotions and wishes which in a given fantasy are associated with specific introjected interpersonal exchanges. They are not endowed with a complex network of mental contents and operations, nor can host meaningfully *inner* conflicts. Rather they represent poles of personality, potentially in conflict with each others. Literary characters cannot and should not be treated or analysed as human beings.

The Author

Literary productivity

A heavy fog
Within my head,
The muscles weak,
The hand iced.

Over the work desk
Too many papers lay and pile.
Deep within
My broken heart waver and dies.

Other psychoanalytically oriented investigations have approached literary works differently, with a focus on a real and specific man or woman: the creative writer. In fact, the psychoanalytic endeavour originated within the framework of clinical work. Psychoanalysis amounts to an attempt to understand real human beings. It is therefore quite natural to make avail of psychoanalysis in order to understand the real person lying behind the text: the author.

This specific style of investigation was never personally pursued by Sigmund Freud with reference to literary creation. However, in *Eine Kindeserinnerung des Leonardos da Vinci* (1910), he applied extensively such approach to the psychoanalytic study of the biography of a major Renaissance painter and scientist.

Freud's interpretation of Leonardo's overwhelming interest for scientific investigation and of his general life organization was based on the analysis of a single memory from Leonardo's infancy, the earlier memory he was able to recollect: "… mi parea che essendo io in culla, che un nibio venissi a me e mi aprissi la bocca colla sua coda e molte volte mi percuotesse con tal coda dentro le labbra" ("it seemed to me that, as I was in my cradle, a kite came on me, opened my mouth by his tail and hit me several times inside my lips by it", *Codice Atlantico*, f. 65). The narrative is obviously unrealistic, and was classed by Freud as a childhood fantasy. Freud believed the kite fantasy gave evidence of enhanced oral drives with substantial homosexual components and concluded his interpretation of the fantasy as follows: "Durch diese erotische Beziehung zur Mutter bin ich einer Homsexualer geworden ("Through this erotic relation to my mother I have become an homosexual", 1910, p. 177).

In his essay on Leonardo, Freud focused his investigation mainly on Leonardo's biographical data. In Freud's view Leonardo lacked significant contact with father in early infancy. This would have fostered an intense and precociously eroticised relation to the mother and allotted his grandmother a particularly important role in his phanatsy life.

Freud illustrated the consequences this peculiar family configuration might have had on Leonardo's development. From our point of view it is important to notice Freud believed it could be an important factor conditioning also his artistic creativity. In particular, he thought that an eroticised relationship to the mother could be the basis for Leonardo's proclivity to represent women with an enigmatic smile, as evidenced by some masterpieces of his, such as *La Gioconda* or *The Virgin and Child with St. Anne,* among others. In Freud's view, the enhanced wish for mother's kisses would have infiltrated the memory of a quietly smiling mother, so introducing a component of tension. The mentioned stylistic feature would then reflect painful responses elicited in Leonardo by the early emotional loss of his mother and at the same time the idealization strategies protecting him from the awareness of this traumatic experience (1910, p. 178 ff.).

In this essay the creative products of an individual were studied in close connection with the artist's biography, in order to produce meaningful hypothesis about his unconscious life. In *Leonardos Kindeserinnerung,* Freud showed how psychoanalysis can explore an artist's life history and fruitfully illuminate its relation to specific artistic creations.

Undoubtedly, the writer appears a proper object of psychoanalytic interest. Greenacre (1955, p. 13) even believed that "the study of the works of a prolific artist offers material as usable for psychoanalytic investigation as the dreams and free associations of the patient".

In fact, Freud's example was followed by many psychoanalysts and critics over the course of XX century. They tried to understand the real person lying behind the text: the author. A massive corpus of studies has been produced within this perspective. We may mention Onorato (1971), Mauron (1950), Miller (1956), Greenacre (1955).

Freud himself, however, was aware that the application of the instruments of psychoanalysis to a painter, surrounded by undisputed admiration of those loving visual arts, could product a shocking effect on the readers. He expressed the fear that his investigation could be perceived as an attempt at demeaning the great man, and felt compelled to state that: "wir Leonardo niemals zu den Neurotikern oder 'Nervenkranken', wo das ungeschickte Wort lautet, gezählt haben" ("we have never reckoned Leonardo as a neurotic or, according to the improper use of the word, as a nerve case", 1910, p. 203). Freud believed a potential hostility among hardcore literary and art critics might arise from the intense idealization phenomenon which surrounds the biography of admired writers or artists and which often underlies vocational choices within the critical domain (1910, pp. 202-203).

Modern literary scholars' hostility against the psychoanalytic interpretation of literary creations depends also on a more field-specific basis. In a sense, psychoanalytic critics continued into the XX century the interest for the artist's life which was so characteristic of romantic criticism (Spitz, 1993, pp. 239 ff.; cfr. Kris, 1952, p. 265). Spitz (1993, p. 240) wrote: "This romantic viewpoint, with its attention centred on the way in which an artist's inner life of feelings finds expression in his works, informed the climate into which Freud's first writings were released".

Around the middle of last century, critical interests moved away from the writer's subjectivity. New criticism (Ransom, 1941) invested more in formal features of the text and tried to emulate the objectivity of natural sciences. From this point of view, psychoanalysis, with its focus on emotion and deep layers of personality, appeared inconsistent with the new critical trends.

Freud had anticipated that the attempt at interpreting and psychoanalytically understanding motives lying under creative activity might endanger or weaken idealization processes so widespread in literary and artistic fruition. However, more recently substantial perplexities about a biographical approach spread also among psychoanalytically informed scholars. They came to realize such investigation strategy entails methodological drawbacks. David Werren (1993, p. 217) has observed that "The inherent problem is that the psychoanalyitic interpretation of a cultural phenomenon lies outside of the therapeutic process in which an interpretation can be inserted...".

The Reader

In contemporary criticism subjective dimensions is not altogether absent, but the focus is no more on the writer's individual experience, rather on the interaction between literary works and the public enjoying them: the readers' not the writers' individuality matters. The Reader Response Criticism (Holland, 1968; Barthes, 1970; Tompkins, 1980) brought into full light the critics' and general public's responses, even emotional responses, to literary works. The new environment offered new opportunities to psychoanalytically oriented critics. Norman Holland (1968) has shown how psychoanalytic devices could usefully be relied upon in order to better understand the emotional reaction a narrative may elicit in the readers.

In fact, a novel or a poem are communicative devices. They generate a relationship located in the social reality, outside the fictitious, narrative environment. They involve an interaction between a writer and the several classes of his readers. The associated exchange of emotions – love, hate, anxiety, pain, desire – takes place on two parallel levels. On the one hand, emotions explicitly reported in the text are re-experienced in the reader's *conscious* experience. On the other hand, underlying, hidden contents are concurrently exchanged.

The process of writing and reading always serves also an *unconscious* communicative function. Any reading of a literary text entails therefore a real emotional interaction, the actual fact of an exchange taking place between individuals.

In Skura's system a *transference related* level of analysis is included. Within this perspective "the exchanges in the psychoanalytic process were taken as a model for the process of reading, which is seen now as an implied exchange between author and reader through medium of the text" (1981, p. 172).

In literary criticism we have access to a text. Through the text we may gain insights into emotionally relevant exchanges which take place between the writer and the reader. Stylistic clues may be observed, which actually may affect the reader's internal world: he may be pained by the suffering of pleasant characters, aroused by the exposition of primal scene material within the text, bored by long and meaningless listings of petty details and so on. A writer may shock or hurt his readers most intimate feelings reporting lethal aggression on children or disfiguring the image of a previously idealised character.

The author can observe directly the emotional impact of his narrative only on a very limited proportion of his readers. But the enormous diffusion of some books actually grants him the power to influence the emotions of maybe millions men and women, of a substantial proportion of humankind. In fact, from this point of view, a literary creation is a medium through which humans carry out emotional interactions on an extraordinary large scale.

The actual (unconscious) interaction between writer and readers can then be a primary focus of the psychoanalytical investigation of literary creation. Object relation theory has developed the necessary framework for such analytical task. The psychoanalytical critic can therefore grasp the main characteristics of this interaction. He may for instance detect the activation of control strategies or seductive operations, or highlight enhanced level of aggression or the gratification of narcissistic needs.

The writer stays outside the direct reach of the psychoanalytic inquiry. Frequently he has long been dead by the time his work is read or however undergoes an analytic interpretation. A lot of information can come from diaries, letters and also material evidence. But the nature of such information, in most cases produced with an eye to a potential future public dissemination, makes it often poorly valuable to a psychoanalytic interpreter.

In case of living authors, discretion needs obviously suggest to abstain from any search for personal biographic data. In fact, the diffusion through public studies of information on a writer's intimate or even unconscious mental life would amount to an improper violation of his or her privacy.

The writer diffuses a creation of his: the work of art. This is the portion of his emotional life he is implicitly willing to share with the public. I believe the work of art and its emotional interaction with the reading public should be a most proper object of critical psychoanalytic study.

In the following Chapter we will discuss this very emotional interaction between writer and readers. We will show how, within the wide span of theoretical perspectives thriving in contemporary psychoanalysis, the interpersonal and intersubjective paradigms are particularly suitable to illuminate the exchanges associated to the reading process.

Chapter Two
The Psychoanalytic Reading of Literary Texts: A Bipersonal Approach

WRITING AS AN INTERPERSONAL ENDEAVOR

Corpus Christi

Your bread
Your body
Your blood

My blood
My pain
My, and yours now

Social animals

Like satellites,
We rotate at a distance,
Inspecting each other
In bewilderment.

Never, though,
We forget
To hit.

In Sigmund Freud's originary understanding of the human mind, emotional events located within the patient's psychic space definitely stood on the foreground. This model, focusing mainly on the patient's isolated mind, has been called intrapsychic. In the course of the development of psychoanalytic theory an increasing awareness of the key role of the interactions between the patient and his main love-obejcts has progressively emerged (Greenberg & Mitchell, 1983).

At the level of the theory of the psychoanalytic process, the advent of such interpersonal paradigm involved a greater appreciation that two people are actually present in the psychoanalytic room: the psychoanalyst no less than the patient (Gill, 1982; Thomä & Kächele, 1985[1990], pp. 20-27). Psychoanalysts relying on the works by Melanie Klein and expanding her theory in the second half of last century displayed a particularly keen interest into the contribution of the psychoanalyst to the psychoanalytic situation.

Among them, Willy and Magdaleine Baranger (1961/62) played a pioneer role and promoted an original conceptualization of the psychoanalytic process as a *sui generis* interpersonal phenomenon. They coined the term *bipersonal field* to the aim of stressing the interactional quality of the emotional scenario enacted by the analyst and the patient. Such dyadic phenomena would stem from thought and emotional process of both participants to the session and, once initiated, would substantially elude the individual control of each of them.

I think this bipersonal approach can be particularly fruitful for a proper psychoanalytic understanding of the literary creative processes. A literary text is obviously not a private fact. It has been written in order to be spread, to be made public. It has been written in order to be read.

The choice to buy a book may be influenced by a number of social factors. Reading literary texts has generally been considered the activity of educated people. It has always been associated to a higher social status. A book may be advertised as responding to socially shared needs, as promoting awareness about political or ethical questions.

However, a book, once bought, still awaits to be read. This will require from the reader the allotment of a significant amount of time: several dozen hours if he is to read a middle-sized novel to its end. I believe reading novels would not be such a common human activity without a strong commitment by the reader (Jackson, 2014, p. 4). So, literary creation – no less than the psychoanalytic process – is actually best conceptualized as a dyadic interaction.

A creative text, every creative text, must have been a contemporary text, before time could bestow it to posterity as a long lasting classic. A text circulates for years or decades during its author's lifetime. A writer has so wide opportunities to physically meet his readers. He actually meets thousand of them through various social events. In addition, he meets a more restricted number of them every day.

Most writers propose their texts to friends and relations before and after the publishing of a book. Commonly, the practice of writing books implies the existence of a restricted audience, an audience whose emotional reactions to the text can actually and immediately reach the writer.

An instance from the life of the greatest German writer may be illuminating. When Goethe (1774) wrote *Die Leiden des jungen Werthers,* he was an emerging literary case. The book met with an overwhelming success and established his standing in literary circles all over Europe. To most readers the intimate connection between the *Werther* plot and Goethe's biography was completely unknown. Goethe however was not unwilling to disseminate personal information. His autobiographical writings spread over several volumes and most of them were published along his lifetime or circulated among fans and admirers.

Actually the greatest German poet in history was able to elicit among contemporaries a keen, nearly voyeristic interest in the detail of his private life. Goethe's affectionate readers came soon to know that Lotte, the main female character in *Die Leiden des jungen Werthers,* was inspired by Charlotte Buff, a real beloved of the writer's. And that the novel triangular plot implicitly replicated the real-life sentimental interaction between Goethe, Charlotte and her then fiancée and later husband Karl Wilhelm Jerusalem. The brief, nostalgic meeting between the now widowed Lotte and the old Goethe, in 1816, was the object of some discreet gossip within Goethe's social circle (Seele, 2000, pp. 49-52). There's no doubt: Lotte had been in a way an absolutely unique reader of *Werther.*

There are, then, readers who are very close to the writer. Their interaction with him may amount to a more or less significant interpersonal relationship. A biographer, particularly a psychoanalytically oriented biographer can find invaluable interpersonal information in novels.

A book, however, travels fast, and long. Even before movable-type printing presses were introduced by Johannes Gutenberg, allowing massive reproductions of books, manuscripts travelled all over Europe and to the East, over sea and waters, and despite the fall of the Roman empire and the chronic war condition of the middle ages reached out to the modern era.

The potential audience of a book is enormous. The absolute majority of readers of any single book will never get in touch with the author neither directly nor by any material or virtual media.

The absolute majority of single readers will never be heard or met by the author. But if we approach the phenomenon of reading as a collective phenomenon, if we focus on readers' reaction as a social group behaviour, readers actually can respond to the stimula the author has included in the text.

The phenomenon of publishing involves the public spreading of an individual's fantasy to a large number of subjects. In fact, each reader is willing to pay a definite amount of money in order to be allowed to share such inner experiences. These fantasies are highly valued. Fantasies are looked for and paid for.

We believe we can understand this enigmatic exchange and the enigmatic value associated to it only if we conceptualize the writer-reader interaction as a *sui generis* interpersonal relationship; and if we are able to characterise the motivational forces and the emotional exchanges underlying such relationship.

To this aim, we may draw substantial benefits from the insights offered by the theory of human relationship developed by Wilfred R. Bion, a highly original psychoanalytic thinker among Melanie Klein's pupils. In Bion's view, human basic emotional experiences emerge within the self in a absolutely primitive, unelaborated state. These precursors of emotional experiences – which Bion termed *ß-elements* – would amount to distinct conglomerates of various emotional reactions elicited during episodes of human interaction (1962, pp. 6-7).

Under optimal conditions, the human mind would be able to contain and transform such raw contents, and ß-elements would then be converted in primary emotional experiences: they could acquire shape and a definite meaning in the subject's inner life, and be detected within the subject's dream activity and neurotic symptoms. This more elaborate experiential material is termed *α-elements* in Bion's language. They would represent the basic bricks of human thought.

However, when an individual's emotional processing resources are exhausted, β-elements can no more be contained within the mental apparatus, and they emerge more directly through manifest behaviours, including self- or object-directed aggression, addictive behaviours, direct activation of the vegetative system (possibly causing various psychosomatic conditions) or a generalized collapse of thought processes (as typically observed in psychotic states).

In Bion's view, core human relationships play a key role in the processing of β-elements. The contribution of people near to us can greatly ease the handling of upsetting emotional experiences.

Typically, the human infant has a very limited ability at processing β-elements. The maintenance of an acceptable well-being in infants is crucially dependent on the ability of the mother to consistently assist the child in processing the contents of his or her emotional experience. The mother's ability to identify and empathise with the infant's emotional and bodily upsetting states is essential in easing the infant's distress. Bion relied on the metaphor of the content/container (1962, pp. 90 ff.), in order to represent this basic function in mother-infant interaction.

In fact, the interpersonal exchange of highly charged emotional experiences lasts much longer than infancy and childhood (Azzone, 2018). It lasts, in various ways, all through the human life. Whilst Melanie Klelin introduced the concept of projective identification as a defence mechanism characterizing the primitive functioning of immature or severely disordered individuals, in Bion's view the exchange of distressing mental contents was a universal and basic device at the root of most core human interactions (1962, p. 31).

Apparently the functioning of the human mind can best be understood in bipersonal terms: the working through of emotions and pain (continuously arising from the unavoidable facts of interpersonal life) can be accomplished only through the interaction between two subjects. The reciprocal process of introducing (actively, or more violently, according to the urgency of the emotional state) emotions and fantasies into the object and being injected with the object's rage, fear, distress, and anxiety, represented, in Bion's thought, the ordinary condition of human couples of any kind (Baranger & Baranger, 1961/62[1990], p. 45).

Pathological development, then, is not produced by the activation of projective identification. Rather, it is the consequence of the object's inability to adequately contain raw emotions and to hand them back to the subject in a more manageable status.

In essence, in order to fully stand the burden of life, men need be able to project negative or too intense emotions in others. This is why humans have socially and historically developed multiple and very effective ways of actively or aggressively forcing emotions into relational objects.

Psychoanalytically oriented clinicians are well aware of the extraordinary power formal features of linguistic communication possess in eliciting intense emotional reactions in the listener. Very slow and detailed descriptions of irrelevant events may induce intense countertransference feelings of rage in the analyst. Prolonged silences can cause a state of extreme annoyance.

Other projective strategies operate more directly on the in-session patient-therapist interaction. In a previous paper I have shown how depressed patients often withdraw from the analyst any clue which could allow him to better understand the relational sources of their suffering. The resulting feelings of absolute helplessness and uselessness are apt to transfer to the analyst particularly distressing experiences of emotional pain (Azzone, 2010).

More developed and articulated emotional constellations may be moved into a relational object through higher order devices. The specific content of a patient's narrative may then be fully exploited. Whether a patient's discourse focuses on real life interpersonal events, on daydreams, or on dream experiences, the selection of general themes may stir powerful emotions in the therapist.

Narrative about sexual relationship or intercourse details may cause jealousy or contertransferential erotic wishes in a therapist of the opposite sex, while eliciting envy in a same sex clinician. A focus on professional achievements may be apt to question a clinician's self esteem, while a report of dangerous or illegal activities may convey a patient's anxieties into the analytic process.

The mentioned examples of active projections of feelings are all drawn from the psychoanalytic situation. Subject and object of projective identification are there in close contact and verbally interacting. However, humans have successfully developed over the centuries highly effective communicative techniques which enable substantial exchange of contents of any kind between individuals or groups at a distance. We reported it above: among such communicational techniques, writing is the oldest one and has shown an extraordinary persistency, in spite of the rapid proliferation of devices for the direct transmission of the human voice and even of real-time images, developments which we behold these very days in front of us.

Writing enables communication at a distance. First of all, at a space distance. In fact, the technique of writing and reading has been developed to the specific aim of enabling men located far from each other to exchange information. A letter can travel thousands of kilometres and reach a reader.

But writing has also an incredible time persistency. A written message can reach a reader after the dust of centuries has covered any remnant of the writer. A relevant proportion of our reading activity is devoted to antique and modern classics, to texts written by men died a long time ago.

Writing is a device serving the needs of human communication. It represents an effective means of emotional interaction. It represents an extraordinary medium for reaching a projective recipient, the world over and through the ages.

Projective identification is an interactive phenomenon. It requires a recipient. Creative writing may offer an obvious comfort to a distressed human: it can promise an author the sharing of a heavy burden, an implicitly but subjectively consolatory ear.

That for the writer, but what can a text offer to the reader? Whenever the content of projective identification is a painful affect, it will cause a corresponding painful emotional state in the object's mind. So, receiving a projective identification is generally painful: it is an unpleasant experience. Humans tend to defend from projections of painful experiences. Intense love, such as the one binding parents to their children, or founding the heterosexual couple, is necessary in order to motivate and sustain humans to accept projections. Psychoanalysts require a professional fee for their qualified availability to accept projections and to help the patient working through their distressing emotional contents. In working life, power and money are often exploited in order to warrant adequate containers to leaders' anxieties and other upsetting emotions.

Reception requires interaction. How can the creative writer obtain listening (or rather reading) for his unconscious misfortunes? How can he overcome "jener Abstossung, die gewiß mit den Schranken zu tun hat, welche sich zwischen jedem einzelnen Ich und den anderen erheben"? ("that repulsion which surely is connected with the boundaries which are established between each Ego and any another one", Freud, 1908a, p. 223). This leads us directly to a long lasting subject of psychoanalytic investigation: which reward can the reader get from the (literary) work of art he is approaching?

Reading involves exposition to another individual's inner world. Sigmund Freud believed that the deepest roots of literary enjoyment had to be found in a parallel wish organization, shared by both reader and writer. They would both host similar unsatisfied wishes of success: in the erotic field, for both sexes, and in terms of social standing for men. In contrast to children, the grown-ups "schämt sich seiner Phantasien" ("are ashamed of their fantasies", *ibidem*, p. 216). Listening or reading a story, men could then identify with the hero's exploits whilst at the same time disavowing the narcissistic and basically megalomanic quality of their own wishes.

In a posthumously published short essay about drama, Freud (1905/6) explicitly admitted narcissistic gratification cannot substantially contribute to the social success of modern psychological, better psychopathological drama. In such circumstances a shared *repressed, unconscious* wish would bind the playwright to his implicitly neurotic audience.

In the last sections of *Der Dichter und das Phantasieren*, however, Freud suggested the writer can also act more subtly to entice potential readers to approach his narrative material. Skilful creative writers could endow competent readers with a wide array of intellectual enjoyments. Linguistic creativity or elegance, complexity of plot and characters' framing, ability to intertwine the narrative with core historical or social issues or philosophical questions: all of that can concur to elicit an aesthetic pleasure. And to have the reader give up his uneasiness towards a stranger's emotional world contents. Freud wrote:

> Man nennt einen solchen Lustgewinn, der uns geboten wird, um mit ihm die Entbindung größerer Lust aus tiefer reichenden psychischen Quellen zu ermöglichen, eine Verlockungsprämie oder eine Vorlust. Ich bin der Meinung, daß alle ästhetische Lust, die uns der Dichter verschafft, den Charakter solcher Vorlust trägt und daß der eigentliche Genuß des Dichtwerkes aus der Befreiung von Spannungen in unserer Seele hervorgeht. (Freud, 1908a, p. 223)

> Such contribution of pleasure – which is offered to us in order to make possible, through it, the release of a greater pleasure, a pleasure stemming from deeper psychic sources – is called a seductive benefit or a preliminary pleasure. I believe that all esthetic pleasure, which the writer provides us with, serves the function of such preliminary pleasure, and that the specific enjoyment drawn from literary works may be traced back to the easing of tensions in our soul.

In essence, writing and reading are concurrent and partly symmetrical processes. Both creative writing and attentive reading are emotionally meaningful activities. They establish an emotional field: a bipersonal field, in fact, where emotions circulate between the writer and each of his readers.

In the present book we will focus our attention also on this very facet of creative writing. We will examine the role creative writing and reading can have in fostering human emotional exchanges. And, more specifically, we will study how men can avail themselves of creative writing to the aim of evacuating, inserting in others or however exchanging highly charged and distressing emotional contents.

UNCONSCIOUS FANTASY AND NARRATIVE TEXTS

Psychoanalytic critics can examine the text of a novel vis-à-vis the reactions stirred by the same novel in themselves and others. Psychoanalysis can be fruitfully applied to the interpretation of the interaction between writer and reader, as it is evidenced by the written text. However, beside this dimension, classified as transference level in Skura's system (1981, pp. 171 ff.), beside actual relations, a novel obviously includes a story, a narrative. This sequence of facts, actually of human interactions, is under our readers' eyes as much as the interaction between the writer and the readers. To be more precise, we may state that the content of the unconscious emotional exchange between writer and reader takes up a basically narrative structure.

Fantasy life is universal in humans. Freud himself – as we reported above – believed a literary work could serve a social function inasmuch as it spoke aloud and publicly generally diffuse conscious fantasies. In his theory of literary creation, Freud focused chiefly on conscious fantasies analogous to the mental activity we commonly refer to as daydreams. He was, however, aware that the unconscious mind is no less keen to fantasy activity.

Unconscious fantasies are mentioned in Freud's works as early as in 1895 (cfr. Laplanche et Pontalis, 1967[2007], p. 153). He was also aware that an unconscious fantasy can play a role in symptom formation (1908b, p. 192-193). However, there can be no doubt that thanks to Melanie Klein the conceptualization of unconscious fantasy reached a unique depth and articulation within the psychoanalytic field. In Klein's perspective, unconscious mind takes up a narrative quality. In her fundamental paper on unconscious fantasy Susan Isaacs – a leading pupil of Klein's – stated that "the primary contents of all mental processes are unconscious phantasies. Such phantasies are the basis of all unconscious and conscious thought processes" (1943, pp. 271-272).

Within Kleinian perspective, human experience is strongly influenced by a number of intrapsychic, highly invested narrative patterns. They are termed fantasies, and the term unconscious fantasy serves to differentiate them from conscious day dreaming activity. In unconscious fantasy core features of mind organization – wishes, anxieties and defenses – are closely interconnected:

> Every impulse, every feeling, every mode of defence is expressed and experienced in such a specific phantasy, which gives it mental life and shows its specific direction and purpose (Isaacs, 1943, p. 278).

Through fantasy the unconscious mind thinks and expresses its "subjective interpretation of experience" (*ibidem*, p. 313). So, in Kleinian thought, unconscious fantasy would include core mental contents and would consistently play an extraordinary role in all or most aspects of mental life: "Phantasy exert *an uninterrupted and omnipresent* influence throughout life, both in normal and neurotic people" (*ibidem*, p. 314).

Fantasy manifests itself in symptoms as well as in dreams, in cultural institutions and values (Segal, 1987; Fornari, 1975; Jaques, 1955; Menzies, 1970; Bion, 1961) and of course in art creations (*e.g.*, Skura, p. 58 ff.; Kanzer, 1950; Milberg-Kaye, 1987). Consistently with this perspective, in the following analysis we will assume unconscious fantasy is a core factor shaping human creative activity and particularly creative writing.

Unconscious fantasy may be conceptualised as an imaginary narrative text. We will assume literary narrative always reflects an underlying unconscious fantasy, an underlying unconscious plot. We believe unveiling such fantasy under the manifest chain of events making up a narrative can be an extremely fruitful endeavour. We believe this approach can offer a viable pathway to the understanding of the motivational forces so widely driving humans to writing and reading stories.

PARTIAL VS. TOTAL OBJECTS IN NARRATIVES

According to Susan Isaacs the importance of unconscious fantasy life persists all through the life cycle. However, different ways of experiencing or structuring fantasies would actually characterize different developmental stages. In early infancy, unconscious fantasy life would be tightly connected to bodily experience, while more articulated visual and then verbal representations of sequential narrative events would appear later on over the course of development:

> [...] the earliest rudimentary phantasy is bound up with sensory experience; it is an affective interpretation of bodily sensations, an expression of libidinal and aggressive impulses, operating under the pressure of the pleasure-pain principle. Later on, phantasy is inherent in sights and sounds, in touch and manipulation and perception of the objects, as well as in gestures and vocal expression, at this stage it is still an *implicit* phantasy.
>
> Still later 'free' images, not 'tied' to actual perception, begin to develop, and phantasy thus become explicit. Much later still some of it may sometimes be expressed in words. [...] In the second year, many phantasies are explicitly acted out in gesture and make-believe play (Isaacs, 1943, p. 288).

Several level of objectual complexity may be identified in the material produced by psychoanalytic patients. It is useful to distinguish within this spectrum two broad categories featuring opposed characters: partial object and total object level unconscious fantasies.

Freud's works on human sexuality assign a decisive role to the shape of human body. In Freud's view instinctual life plays a key role in the development of humans and in their emotional life. Basic instincts – hunger, sexual drive and the wish of getting rid of residues of digestion and catabolism – would heavily condition the self-representation of human body.

Bodily surfaces and openings which are connected with these basic functions would receive a massive investment – a massive libidinal cathexis in Freud's language. In fact Freud correctly perceived that areas involved in eating, excretion and coital activity are the object of an extraordinary attention in all societies. Basic social norms regulate these activities everywhere. For excretory and genital area severe interdictions of display in public context is shared by all antique and modern civilizations (*cfr*. Douglas, 1966).

Freud also regarded the oral, anal and genital areas as an inexhaustible source of representative material for psychopathology (Freud, 1905 & 1923). Typically, hysterical or obsessive symptoms or character traits would allude to the gratification of any such erogenous zones (*e.g.*, Freud, 1916). Parts of the human body involved in such libidinal activities have an enormous importance in Freud's conceptualization of the unconscious mental life.

Within this model child sexuality would go through three basic steps. The earliest libidinal drives would revolve around feeding functions and the related anatomical structures. The wish to be nurtured would make then mouth and lips a locus of highly invested oral pleasure. During toilet training adults' attention gets focused on the child ability and willingness to comply with their expectations for order and cleanliness. Later on in the developmental process, according to Freud's formulation in *Die infantile Genitalorganisation* (1923), libidinal cathexis gets focused on the male genital. Freud termed this developmental stage the phallic phase.

From this stage onward, the male penis would stand out as a core organizer of emotional development. Most of human sexuality-related fantasy life would revolve around the representation of this single body part. Consistently, the core task in male psychosexual development would be the management of castration anxieties (Freud, 1908c). The little boy would confront the annihilating fears arisen by the all powerful father, the expected punishment for the implicit longing to establish himself as a potential partner and libidinal object for family females, including mother. The father's retaliation for each son's striving towards the mother would be the core danger in the interpersonal and intrapsychic constellation Sigmund Freud termed the Oedipus complex.

Consistently with such view of the human development, partial objects were frequently mentioned in Freud's interpretations. Their role got even wider in the thought and practice of an outstanding pupil of his: Melanie Klein. For the Hungarian borne psychoanalyst partial objects were the basic components of early infants' fantasy life. In Kleinian perspective early psychic life is dominated by a configuration of wishes, fears and defences which she termed schizoparanoid position (*cfr.* Klein, 1952). At this stage object relations are characterized by a) aggressive and sadistic wishes towards the maternal object and b) fears of retaliatory attacks from the same object or the combined parental couple.

In the schizoparanoid position objects are typically represented as partial objects. Fanatsy life consists mainly of narratives reporting interactions between body parts: breast/milk/mouth, rectum/ faeces, penis/vagina, rather than people (father/mother/son/daughter).

In Klein's conceptualization, normal or however non psychotic development would be closely dependent on the overcoming of the schizoparanoid position and the access to a more mature internal object configuration: the depressive position. A distinguishing feature of this developmental shift would be the appearance of more elaborated intrapsychic object narratives. The various object aspects, components or parts are now integrated in a complex, multifaceted *total* object.

The Kleinian school is particularly keen on the psychoanalytic investigation of the deepest layers of the mental organization, with a parallel interest in the treatment of young children and severe, even psychotic cases. Consistently with such attitude, Melanie Klein and the psychoanalysts relying on her conceptualization of unconscious mind acknowledged to partial objects a unique role in the formulation of interpretations.

This excerpt from the analysis of Richard, a 10 years old schoolboy suffering from depressive mood and agoraphobia may illustrate such interpretative style:

> In my interpretation I linked this fear with the 'pig-sty' town; it stood in his mind for my 'inside' and his mother's 'inside', which had turned bad because of thunderstorms and Hitler's bombs [Klein was back from a trip to London. Sessions took place during World War II]. These represented his 'bad' father's penis entering his mother's body and turning it into an endangered and dangerous place. The 'bad' penis inside his mother was also symbolized by the poisonous toadstools which had grown in the garden in my absence, as well as by the monster against which the little man (representing himself) was fighting. The phantasy that his mother contained the destructive genital of his father accounted in part for his fears of sexual intercourse. This anxiety had been stirred up and intensified by my going to London. His own aggressive wishes relating to his parents' sexual intercourse greatly added to his anxieties and feelings of guilt (Klein, 1945, p. 375).

In Kleinian interpretative style the disguised allusion to body parts included in the narratives told by the patient are spelled out in detail. Through a proper translation work the underlying narrative is exposed to the patient.

Contrary to the manifest content of the patient's material, this underlying narrative speaks about bodily events rather than object interactions. In fantasy the patient suckle his or her mother's breast, bites, or even devours her, smears her with stinking faecal material or feels trapped in mother's or father's rectum along with faeces, watches enraged the parents' coitus or longs to substitute the father or mother in his or her marital role. Exposure to partial object experiences can leave unaffected none of us, as the reader has surely experienced this very moment in reading the previous lines.

As the clinical excerpt clearly testifies, Melanie Klein focused her attention on the intense, flooding emotions associated with the bodily narratives. Body parts appealed to her inasmuch as they allowed to reconstruct highly charged interpersonal interactions with a patient's core objects.

In fact, reliance on partial objects as core components of interpretative activity does not drive attention away from the specifically human dimension of interpersonal life. Rather, it retains and conveys the primitive and powerful emotions elicited by interpersonal and particularly intrafamilial relationships in the inner world.

Consistently, the reconstruction of human relationships in terms of bodily interactions can be particularly helpful to the psychoanalytic investigation only inasmuch as it allows the unveiling of basic and primitive emotions stirred by human relations. The sole identification of symbols of bodily parts within a patient's material would actually amount to a vain effort.

Lists of penises, breasts, nipples, vaginae, mouths, anuses, cannot as such enrich our understanding of human suffering and experience, should they be devoted of the relevant anger, arousal, envy, love, hate, greed, and so on. This attitude is definitely sterile in the clinical setting, but even more so in the field of applied psychoanalysis. Skura (1981, p. 70-71) states:

> The psychoanalytic critic has never had much trouble identifying the "specular" fantasy repetitions of the manifest story - a series of analogy going back to childhood, floating somewhere in the background of the story [...]. He has had less success in incorporating these phantoms into the body of the work and reconciling what he finds with what the ordinary reader thinks to be the text. [...] the tension between the manifest and the latent fantasy is then said to explain all the text's ambiguities, all the conflicts and tensions which the ordinary reader detects

In fact, the first generation of psychoanalytic critics, possessed by the enthusiasm for Freud's discoveries, offered to the literary community cold lists of partial objects, so consistently depriving the literary material of the emotional and narrative wealth it contained. Jones (1923) equates any dwarf who is met in myth, folklore, or literature with a penis. Reviewing Edgar Allan Poe's short story *The purloined letter,* Marie Bonaparte (1935) showed no hesitation in discovering female genital symbolism in Mr. Dupin's fireplace. Norman

Holland (1968, pp 107-114) reads the celebrated, highly iconic metaphor of life as a nonsense theatre performance which embellishes Shakespeare's *Macbeth* as a straightforward spelling out of the primary scene. We can fully understand, against this background, the bitter acceptance they received by professional critics.

Such hostility had an obvious impact on more recent psychoanalytic critics. They tried to prevent a parallel angry reception by keeping their investigations as free as possible from allusion to primitive body representations.

We may mention Barbara Freedman (1987), Rivka R. Eifermann (1993) and the now classic Lacan's seminar on *The Purloined letter* (1966) as examples from the wide range of more recent psychoanalytic approaches to literature. Focus is now on interpersonal relationships, on narcissistic issues and defence mechanisms. These reading styles rely mostly on total object approaches for the interpretation of the text. This critical stance has undoubtedly been fruitful and has offered readers and professional critics alike new perspective on literary creation and literary texts.

However, I believe we should be more aware of the consequences an exclusive reliance on a total object approach may have on the aims and scope of the psychoanalytically oriented study of literary texts. Partial objects are the peculiar inhabitants of the world of primitive unconscious fantasies. They amount to the building bricks of early child fantasy life and indeed to the alphabet in which core and primitive emotional experiences are spelled out over the entire course of our life.

Abstinence from identification and interpretation of partial objects narratives underlying literary works may represent a consistent methodological option, but unavoidably yields a depleted, one-sided representation of the analysed texts. In fact, the emotional resonance of a literary narrative in the reader's inner world is likely to depend closely on the writer's ability to weave a narrative web which includes highly invested emotional issues. And psychoanalysis has widely shown over the past century that primitive fantasies reflecting core bodily experiences in relations with love-objects are very likely to be the most intense representations of experiences available to most or all humans. If the psychoanalytic study of creative texts is to gain a meaningful insight into the basic motivational forces driving humans all over the world to read novels, it cannot easily give up the task of identifying partial object fantasies included in the texts.

However, psychoanalysis can widen and deepen the general experience of reading novels only inasmuch as body part identification is fully exploited as a mean to reconstruct relations. Bodily events – child delivery, suckling, biting, eating, expelling, retaining, inserting, receiving, kissing, humming – reflect and magnify emotions elicited by *object relations*. Body parts enliven our understanding of creative writing if they can retain the awful intensity of emotions arising within early object relations.

From a methodological point of view, the psychoanalytic exploration of creative texts may be meaningful only inasmuch as it can offer evidence of a specific tie between emotional and cognitive contents in the manifest text, unconscious representations of bodily events and a specific interpersonal conflict associated with enhanced rage, fear or jelousy. Only a substantial consistency within these differing narrative levels can offer significant support to any particular interpretative hypothesis. In a recent essay (Azzone, in press) we have shown how a psychoanalytically informed reading of a medieval chivalric romance can unveil this very parallel and cross-fertilization between deep primitive and interpersonal levels of analysis.

Chapter Three
Methodological Issues

As reported above, identification of partial objects within literary or however creative material has been often judged a highly arbitrary endeavour, where the critic's theoretical background deeply affects the outcome of the investigational task. We therefore believe we'd better make as explicit as possible to the reader methods and procedures we will be relying upon in our reading of Dan Brown's *The Da Vinci Code*.

In the following sections we will outline specific procedures which can allow a psychoanalytic reader to detect and characterize partial object relations within a literary narrative. We will illustrate our options by the discussion of some literary texts.

MATERIAL SELECTION

In *Die Traumdeutung* (1900, p. 289) Freud introduced the concept of overdetermination. Any product of mental activity – he argued – contains multiple layers of meaning. Every human event is concurrently experienced by different levels of personality and is processed concurrently by mature and infant-like level defence strategies. This obviously extends to any creative text.

A narrative is bound to transfer to the reader multiple levels of meaning: realistic representations of parental imagos, authority conflicts, triangular jealousy conflicts, but also paranoid fears, primitive idealization and – not the least – frightening or alluring bodily interactions.

From the point of view of the application of psychoanalysis to literary texts, we are therefore confronted with the need to select narrative segments which are likely to include abundant early fantasy material and to harbour interactions between partial objects.

To this aim we must first of all focus our attention on shapes of men, animals, objects as represented in the text. At this level, we must be able to forget living beings' identity or names. The narrative builds up a complex and articulated world in front of us. Within this context, we need look at it as a collection of heterogeneous shapes.

Within a partial object perspective, landscape is frequently interpreted as a representation of the human body, most typically mother's (e.g. Jackson, 2014, p. 80-81). In the shapes of buildings, clothing articles, vegetables, animals, the characters' body (Lewin, 1933), or characters' gestures, we will look for analogies with the anatomical shape of the human body: curves, dips, prominences.

The plastic shapes the writer's pen is able to paint in front of us may be specified further by information from other sensory channels. Visual imagery may be profitably supplemented by reported sounds, smells, tastes, tactile perceptions, which all may contribute important clues, drawing our attention to the possible presence in the material of elements representing body parts.

Obviously, a literary text is made up of words. Words refer to objects in reality or in fantasy world. However, ever since his *Traumdeutung* (1900, *e.g.*, pp. 110 ff.) and all through the course of his scientific career, Freud has been aware that words may include – and at the same time conceal – allusions to repressed contents. These allusions may be very useful also with reference to our specific investigative endeavour, and bring support to morphologically based interpretative hypotheses. We will show later to the reader that the text we will analyse in the present essay features an unusual abundance of linguistic clues to disguised unconscious contents.

Search and identification of partial objects are important steps in the evaluation of narrative texts. Availability of narrative segments including abundant primitive fantasy material is a basic perquisite for the reading style we are here purporting.

Memories hosted in each human's mind cannot obviously be counted. Unconscious fantasies are emotional traces of intense object relational experiences. Their number, too, exceeds the reach of our understanding. Also within the more restricted boundaries of a literary text, multiple unconscious plots may accommodate themselves. Unconscious fantasies may shape the narration of short sequences of events reported in a few text pages, and may at the same time surface in a novel general narrative structure. We may not proceed to text analysis as long as such sequences have not been disentangled.

Unconscious fantasy is the mental record of an emotional experience: the sequence of emotional responses which have been carved in the wax table of a human mind by a sequence of interpersonal events. Real life interpersonal experiences have a beginning and unroll over time. They take place at a specific time and in a specific place. An unusually pleasant conversation with an old rival or an anger crisis at the end of a quarrel with wife are discrete interpersonal events. Their time limits can be clearly identified. They surely elicit conspicuous emotional responses, which on turn are stored within the subject's mind as distinct unconscious fantasies.

Unconscious narratives disseminated through literary texts must then possess parallel identifiable borders. Under a general perspective, internal consistency is the basic criterion which the psychoanalytic reader may rely upon in order to extract discrete narratives from the general text flow. A sequence of events in the text may be usefully woven into a common narrative framework inasmuch as they all allude to a single and coherent system of meanings.

Once the reader has identified these as core features of the narrative, he can identify all the events in the text which have significant ties with the theme. We may illustrate the point through an example from Dan Brown's bestseller. While reading *The Da Vinci Code,* the reader may choose to focus on the manhunt theme. In *The Da Vinci Code* manhunt by a dangerous and initially unknown persecutor amounts to an overarching narrative structure. The hunt begins at Chapter 18 with Prof. Langdom's flight from the Louvre Museum, and ends with Lord Teabing's arrest at Chapter 101.

Within these limits, the segments of the text to be selected for analyses should include all narrative material which contains information relevant to the identified issue, in this example with the manhunt of Prof. Langdom: reasons for the hunt, hunters and prey's qualities, all emotions elicited by this specific situation in the characters according to the text, the consequences of the hunt, and the final outcome.

For the selection of material relevant to the specific identification of part-objects narratives the reader may rely on the same general guidelines, but the unique features of this narrative material warrant the adoption of some specific strategies. In fact part object narratives are warded off more attentively by the writer's and the readers' censorships. Objects described in the text as material objects are often exploited by the unconscious mind with the aim of representing parts of the living human body.

In order to properly assess the narrative consistency of the selected material the reader need therefore focus on the unconscious meaning included in the text. The reader should try to distance himself from surface material and to concentrate his attention on possible representatives of bodily events.

A basic step in the segmentation of material is then the identification of disguised representations of bodily interactions between human beings. Consistently with Freud's general theory of human libidinal (*i e* drive related) activities, those bodily interactions between humans may be conceptualized through the metaphors of nutrition, excretion and genital union.

First of all, the psychoanalytic reader will scan the material for the identification of related symbols of part-objects. Then he will try to get an insight into the fantasy interactions organized around such body part representatives. He will try to grasp the peculiar qualities of these interactions and to ascertain whether they can be assigned to the oral, anal or genital domain.

He will finally review the internal consistency of the material and try to identify under the manifest content coherent sequences of bodily interactions with the associated emotions. A segment may be judged appropriate for the subsequent analyses only in as much as all disguised allusions to the identified bodily interactions may be articulated in a meaningfully body related narrative.

FORMULATION OF THE PARTIAL OR TOTAL OBJECT UNCONSCIOUS FANTASY

As we have illustrated above the potential for intense emotional communication implicit in an unconscious fantasy can be disclosed to the reader only inasmuch as the full span of both cognitive and affective contents of the partial or total object relationship narrative is retained in the reading process. The psychoanalytically oriented reader is called therefore to a two-step process: a) the identification of the unconscious (fantasmatic) content of the textual material and b) the understanding of the quality and intensity of the interpersonally elicited emotions associated with the material in the text.

First of all, the reader should characterize the general nature of the objects included in the fantasy: human beings versus body parts. The knowledge of common fantasy themes in healthy or psychologically ill individuals will help him to identify narrative contents. And to grasp possible parallels, overlapping or rather peculiarities versus socially prevailing drive and fear constellations.

Total object fantasies can be usefully clustered with reference to their relationship with the Oedipus complex. In earlier or more primitive phantesies, distress (or blessing) arises in the interaction between two people: wishes of fusion, intimacy, closeness, dependence, narcissistic investment tend to prevail in such material, as well as fears of aggression, rejection, coldness, indifference.

On the other hand, material conditioned by the activation of the Oedipus complex features more articulated triangular interactions. In the Oedipal configuration the basic wish is obviously that of securing the possess of the contested love-object. In heterosexual relationship, sexual union is the behavioural event factually attesting the unrestricted availability of the love-object. In other relationships, various privileges bestowed by parents, relatives, friends, physicians, co-workers, or office-heads can give evidence of the longed for preference by the object.

In organizations, Oedipal configurations do not necessarily reflect hierarchic structure. Subordinate workers may sometimes occupy the vertex of the Oedipal scenario and compliance with the head's expectations, initiatives, or even philosophy can also be ways for gratifying or frustrating Oedipal wishes. The core feature of Oedipal wishes is more generally the possess of the object to the exclusion of any possible competitor.

To a mind mainly functioning at an Oedipal level the interpersonal world tend to appear inhabited by either potentially libidinal objects or dangerous rivals. The wish to attest his own superiority to them is then pervasive and jealousy is the basic anxiety.

Freud believed certain experiences exerted a traumatic impact which was to last all through development and beyond. He termed them *Urszenen* ("primal scenes"; in a note of 1897, cfr. M. Bonaparte, A. Freud & E. Kris, 1950, p. 210), and later on *Urphantasien* ("primal fantasies", 1915, p. 242). The core traumatic event in the Oedipal constellation is the exposure to the parents' sexual union: the primal scene *par excellence* in contemporary psychoanalytic terminology (Freud, 1918, p. 63 ff.). In fantasy narrative, anxiety with reference to an interacting couple may often attest to a basic Oedipal conflict.

The identification of *partial objects level fantasy* requires a greater technical subtlety. In general, the events involving the story characters are here poorly informative with reference to the actual nature of the underlying unconscious fantasy. Character's emotions, wishes and anxieties can be useful to the psychoanalytic understanding of a text concealing a primitive fantasy only inasmuch as the reader is able to bring to light and individually characterize the body part symbols dispersed within the text flow. The novice reader will be startled to discover the extraordinary consistency that even apparently chaotic narrative texts can acquire as soon as the web of partial objects meanings have been reconstructed.

To the efforts by Sigmund Freud we owe a basic classification of human drives (*Drei Abhandlungen der Sexualthorie,* 1905). Within Freudian conceptualization of human motivational forces, wishes are assigned a necessary and definite sexual quality. An intense discharge of sexual energy is assumed to be yielded by the stimulation of bodily orifices.

Motivational development in infancy and early childhood would then progress across three distinct steps, the oral, anal and phallic stages. In the oral stage suckling plays a core role in ensuring the child's attachment to mother and allowing nutritional exchanges between mother's and child's bodies.

Oral stage fantasy material is dominated by the somatic partners of such feeding processes: the mouth and the breast. Their lingering under the manifest narrative can be inferred from human or environmental morphology. Spheres, celestial bodies, hills may conceal allusions to the breast. Openings of various kinds may betray an oral character when provided with points or blades or represented as enveloping or trapping, or when characteristic tastes are underlined in the text. Dogs or other carnivores may involve oral allusions. According to Sigmund Freud, a typical oral level drive is the wish to incorporate the breast, *i.e.* eating it (1905, p. 98). In narrative material this wish is commonly assigned to the object and experienced in terms of fear. The flight from the jaws of a wild animal is a topos in adventure novels and comics.

Later on in development does Freud locate prevailing anal strivings. Anal level libidinal fantasies would feature a bipolar quality. They would allude to both autoerotic anal stimulation and faecal retention, to both active and passive homosexual wishes. Within narrative material a typical clue is the entrance into or the exit out of a key chasm. Such critical doors or openings are typically carefully warded and access is uncomfortable. Castle draw-bridges or gatehouses may be good examples. For instance, in *The Da Vinci Code* a particularly attentive procedure regulates the access to the vault of the Swiss Bank (Chapter 42).

A clue to the anal quality of a narrative sequence may be offered by unpleasant smells from any source as well as by a general feeling of uneasiness or shame, as we will show below through an example from a French mediaeval romance.

In his *Drei Abhandlungen zur Sexualthorie* (1905, p. 99), Freud stated aggression is a significant component also in anal stage sexual drives. He explicitly noted the enjoyment the subject can draw form the object's suffering (1905, p. 60). In anal stage narrative material this eroticised sadistic component may be apparent.

According to the *Drei Abhandlungen* the child's psychosexual development completes around five years of age but centrality of the genitals would be established only at puberty:

> [...] in Kinderjähren eine Objektwahl vollzogen wird, [...] in der Weise, daß sämtliche Sexualbestrebungen die Richtung auf eine einzige Person nehmen, an der sie ihre Ziele erreichen wollen. Dies ist dann die größte Annährung an die definitive Gestaltung des Sexuallebens nach der Pubertät, die in den Kinderjähren möglich ist. Der Unterschied von letzerer liegt nur noch darin, daß die Zusammenfassung der Partialtriebe und deren Unterordnung unter das Primat der Genitalien in der Kindheit nicht oder nur sehr unvollkommen durchgesetzt wird (p. 100).

> In childhood an object choice is completed, ... which means that sexual desires as a whole get attached to a single person, on whom they focus their aims. This is the closest approximation to the definitive configuration of sexual life after Puberty, which is possible in infancy. The difference from the former lies only in that in childhood the coalescence of partial drives under the primacy of the genitals is not reached at all or only to a limited extent.

In later works (*i.e.*, 1923) Freud introduced the concept of phallic organization – basically autoerotic and dominated by castration anxieties – as the terminal stage of child sexual development. He believed that only the achievement of somatosexual maturation in early adolescence would allow male and female to associate their sexual drives to heterosexual coupling fantasies.

From our point of view, it is useful to identify possible textual clues to the union of male and female genitals. A basic graphic element of genital level narrative is the entrance of a literary character into an environment, most typically a building. The differentiation from situations implying a more anal character may be eased by allusions to cleanliness, transparency or any kind of lubrications. The presence of water is a pervasive clue. The association of a tree and a spring or a lake is a prototypical element of innumerable literary (*e.g.*, Chrétien de Troyes, *Le chevalier au lion*, vv. 368-427) folkloric (e.g., *The Devil with the Three Golden Hairs*, from brothers Grimm's *Children's and Household Tales,* 1812/1815, KHM 29*)* and mythological (*e.g.*, the location and ritual of the temple of Diana Nemorensis at Nemi, as reported by Frazer, 1890, I, p. 1-4) landscapes. In Freud's *Traumdeutung* (1900, pp. 355 - 410) the reader can find a comprehensive discussion of common narrative representatives of various body parts and particularly the genitals, with many examples from both dreams and neurotic patients' clinical material.

At a genital developmental level heterosexual intercourse comes to be highly cathected, even the object of an excruciating pervasive longing. In literary texts this may surface in the intensity of a character's effort to get access into a space. A duel or a fight with a competitor or opponent may be a revelatory feature. In the man-woman relation, a typical interaction may include rejection, especially when associated to devaluation. Marked anxiety about any kind of physical or intellectual performance has always been interpreted in terms of castration anxiety within the psychoanalytic tradition. In the widely known Russian folktale *The Feather of Finist the Falcon* (Afanasajev, 1873, n. 234-235) the hawk lover is severely wounded when entering his beloved's bedroom window. The term "vagina dentata" has been introduced in the psychoanalytic jargon (Rank, 1924, pp. 48-49) to indicate a widespread theme in myths and folklore (Otero, 1996), which blends oral and genital features.

In Chrétien de Troyes' *Le Chavalier de la Charrette* we read how Lancelot, in his steadfast effort to get access to the imprisoned Ginevra's room, walks barefooted upon a blade (vv. 3017- 3115) and tears open barehanded a window grating (vv. 4633 - 4646). So his hands and feet are injured, and when enjoying the queen's reward he unwittingly smears her bedding linen with revelatory blood spots (vv. 4698 – 4701).

We have offered the reader an essential review of some typical symbolization patterns. We add that, to the aim of formulating fruitful hypothesis about the bodily experience underlying a literary text, associative imaginery is as much or even more helpful than any systematisation attempt.

We cannot propose empirical methods for testing or falsifying this kind of literary reading hypothesis. As I mentioned earlier, a subjective but productive criterion may be that of assessing the narrative consistency of the unconscious bodily narrative the reader has been able to construe. Narrative sequences which are consistent with physiologically and psychologically meaningful patterns are more likely to yield productive hypotheses about the examined material.

Bodily Events and Interactions in the Interpersonal Space

In the previous section we have repeatedly underscored partial objects' detection is only the first step in the psychoanalytic reading and interpretation of a literary text. Bodily interactions are universal. They are experienced both fantasmatically and concretely by all humans. Their presence in a literary text is in a sense unavoidable and may then *per se* be trivial.

Understanding the underlying partial object material can enhance our ability to identify and share contents with a communicating subject (including a writer communicating through a creative text) only inasmuch as the emotional reality associated to this bodily interactions can be fully elucidated.

The human mind relies so much on partial object fantasies due to their enormous potential for freeing – and conveying to the listener or reader – primitive emotions. On the other hand, most intense emotions commonly arise within interpersonal relations.

The psychoanalytic reader identifies fantasies within a literary text. He maps narrative events to bodily interactions. His most rewarding – albeit arduous – task is that of fully illuminating the nature of the relational experience which has generated the unconscious fantasy.

The partial object material can show him the core quality of the human events at issue. It is apt to disclose the conflict around which the fantasy subject is struggling about: love vs. hate, dependence vs. autonomy, control vs. freedom, self-efficiency vs. helplessness, openness vs. closure, exploitation vs. reciprocity.

Partial objects allow the reader to grasp the basic interpersonal axis eliciting the unconscious fantasy lying under the manifest text. The manifest narrative, on its turn, allows the reader to understand and qualify the interpersonal characters and the emotional responses associated to the fantasy interaction.

A writer can give life to characters only inasmuch as he is able to identify with them to an extent. In fact, Freud believed that behind each and every character in dreams, nothing else than the dreamers' Ego lay in disguise (1900, p. 327-328). Each dream character is embedded in parts of the dreamer's personality. This is obviously true also for narrative texts.

Through projective identifications, all human are incessantly exchanging roles in relationships. However, life as well as clinical experience easily teach us that any individual unconsciously selects a preferred pole in interactions. Masochists are clearly not at ease when forced to subsume a sadistic role.

In order to understand and spell out a fantasy we need to specify the main identification of the narrating subject. We must ascertain whether the narrating subject identify mainly with the victim or the harasser, with the seducer or the seduced, with the dependent child or the caring parent and so on.

Luckily, grasping the subject's position in a narrative is generally an easy task. The main character in a novel or a novel segment can reasonably be supposed to play out needs, wishes and emotions of the unconscious fantasy subject. Similarly, when a story is told by a narrating persona, he is likely to voice the fantasy subject's feelings and thoughts. For instance, with reference to *The Da Vinci Code*, which will be the focus of the psychoanalytic reading reported in the second part of the book, the narrator's viewpoint is obviously identified with Prof. Langdon's. Similarly, in the shorter subnarrative of Silas's early life recollections, the regressive need to be cared for by the bishop Aringarosa may be safely associated with the narrating subject.

Once the psychoanalytical reader has identified the quality of the main object relationship in a narrative and the character representing the subject in the text, he has got all the elements which can help him to reach a comprehensive understanding of the unconscious fantasy. In fact, in most cases, affects are expressed in fantasy material in an explicit fashion. The unconscious mind resorts to complex disguising devices in order to conceal the nature of the interactions which tantalise it and the real objects involved in them. But more easily acknowledges and shares the affects elicited by such relations.

Commonly, the reader can find them directly expressed in the text. They are open to the curiosity of any critical approach and to any reader's unprejudiced enjoyment attitude towards the text. They are the main character's emotions.

The psychoanalytic reader is in the unique and luckily position to articulate these emotional responses against the complex and often bewildering background of the object relationship from which they arise.

LOOKING FOR PARTIAL OBJECTS:
TWO EXAMPLES FROM MEDIEVAL CHIVALRIC LITERATURE

Partial object identification has always been a prominent and socially conspicuous feature of psychoanalytic interpretation of literary texts. It has been able to upset *fin de siècle* puritan audiences as well as to elicit the sounder skepticism of academics from a more specific literary background. In fact, too often a stereotyped and somewhat sickening search for symbolic representatives of penis, breast or anus has replaced a comprehensive understanding of the full span of unconscious emotional contents underlying the text. This sterile and simplistic investigational stance cannot meaningfully contribute to the understanding of literary texts, works of art, folkloric narratives and religious beliefs and rituals. Rather, it usually yields highly conjectural and generic lists of partial object or conflicts. It typically exposes in the material universal unconscious themes, lacking any specific tie to the investigated material.

Specificity, in fact, is the basic question. The main perquisite for a meaningful and productive psychoanalytic approach to literary texts is the ability to unveil the specific unconscious fantasy it thrives on: the network of highly conflictual object relations and associated fear and defences, the conglomerate of primitive conflicting unconscious emotions which represents the motivational basis for the author's compelling creative drive and for the no less greedy fruition of his work by the readers.

From this point of view, we need give evidence of a specific correspondence between manifest emotional and cognitive content of the text, unconscious representations of bodily events and a specific unconscious interpersonal conflict laden with rage, fear and jealousy. Consistency between contents yielded by these three layers of meaning may give substantial support to any suggested interpretative hypothesis.

In order to better illustrate our interpretative approach we will now offer the reader an analysis of two literary texts, two short segments from works by Chrétien de Troyes: the scene of the Chastel de la Pesme Avventure (the "Castle of the Foul Adventure" from *Le Chevalier au Lion*) and the scene of the Liz de la Merveille (the "Bed of the Wonder") which ends the *Conte du Graal*.

Text I: Le Chastel de la Pesme Avventure
(*Le Chevalier au Lion*, vv. 5103-5768)

Two male characters stand out within the plot of the *Yvain*: beside the Chevalier au Lion, we find Gauvain, his best friend. The romance tells the story of a male friendship where increasing tension arises in two interpersonal areas: Yvain's wife's jealousy and the overlap and confusion of roles and identities between the two knights. Their friendship is sound but chivalric etiquette leads them unwittingly to a mortal combat. The intense object relationship between two males bogs down in a conflict and haughty competition between the twin-like couple members.

Love for the identical endangers the narcissistic representation of a powerful and admired Self. Intense interaction with the male brings the risk of a psychical and physical submission: it's a direct threat to manhood.

The reported role conflicts, lingering within the manifest content of the novel, will now guide our search for the unconscious fantasy underlying the selected text. We will consequently try to detect possible bodily interactions consistent with the identified main object relationship issue, *i.e.* homosexual interactions between males. We will now report a brief summary of the episode of the Chastel de la Pesme Avventure.

At sunset Yvain notices a unknown castle and makes up his mind to spend the night there. The faithful lion and a maid follow him. The locals shout abuse at him: if he gets into the castle he will be worth of the utmost contempt. Yvain tries to reply, to defend his choice, but is forced to admit:

> \- Dame, fait il, Dix le vous mire!
> Mais mes faus cuers laiens me tire,
> Si farai che que mes cuers vuet (vv. 5171-5173)

> \- Madam, may God save you!
> But my false heart leads me there,
> Therefore I will do what my heart wants

The Chevalier au Lion passes the drawbridge and enters a wide lobby. Along the walls, between vertical logs, a series of maiden sits sewing. They are dressed only in tattered, worn out rags. The maidens lament their miserable fate and Yvain expresses his sympathy. Yvain's attempt to leave the castle is promptly repelled by the doorkeeper.

Through a little door he then enters a garden. There the lord and the lady of the castle greet him, while their daughter is reading aloud a romance. The emotional climate is courtly, cheerful, and pleasant.

The following morning things appear changed. The lord of the castle makes known to Yvain that he will not be allowed to leave the castle unless he fights and wins two devils, sons of Neptune and a mortal woman. They are ugly, hideous beings, featuring a primitive bizarre attire. Yvaine's arms are helpless against their superhuman strength. Only the unexpected intervention of the faithful lion saves him.

Now the devils lie dead. The lord of the castle is willing to betroth his daughter to him. Yvain resists his urgent proposal and leaves the castle.

"Honte", "lait": the abuse addressed to Yvain on his way to the Chastel de la Pesme Aventure marks out the specific emotion pervading this narrative segment and implicitly the associated unconscious bodily interaction: this emotion is shame. An obvious conflict is sketched between an overwhelming drive ("I will do what my heart wants") and a serious threat to the narcissistic self-representation.

The scene of the lobby of the castle (vv. 5187-5325) features an extraordinary representational efficacy. Chrétien positions the unfortunate maidens around a central space, between wooden logs. Rounded bodily parts protrude from tattered rags. Chrétien represents the perineal area with an amazing anatomical detail. He even includes the prolapse of sphincteral tissues and hemorrhoidal plexuses.

However, access to the most intimate area of the castle is an arduous task. Yvain experiences deep pain and genuine concern for the object, but he is bound to proceed further. Within this inner, core space climate is somewhat elated: luxury, fine clothes, literature and an exquisite dinner, but soon anxiety surfaces again.

Devils feature a bizarre and complex shape, where anal (black color) and phallic (the shield on the head) traits freely merge with each other. Yvain is compelled to renounce the support of his lion: his manhood frightens the object.

However, castration anxiety soon proves too intense: Yvain is helpless in front of the giants and faces death. The faithful lion escapes from the room it has been locked up in, a devil turns around and Yvain can now hit him from behind. Yvain is now the winner, and the way back from the castle is safe and easy.

In the episode of the castle, themes and relational conflicts which are included in the manifest text are represented through an accurate system of biunivocal relations. Both in the novel manifest plot and in the unconscious fantasy which underlies the selected segment, a sexual interaction between males is at issue. However the unconscious fantasy bestows us the access to a definitely more intense emotional material. Shame, guilt feelings, arousal, wish, dread of submission, the immediate threat of a narcissistic collapse, take on an iconic evidence which neither the manifest text nor any theoretical analysis could in any way hand over to the reader.

Text II. Le Liz de la Merveille (*Le Conte du Graal*, vv. 7140-8287)

In the *Conte du Graal,* the relationship between the male and the female is a core dimension both in the manifest content and in the unconscious fantasy (Azzone, in press). From the romance we have selected the following narrative segment, where abundant partial object material consistent with such hypothesis can be detected.

Gauvain reaches the bank of a wide and deep river. Due to a wicked maiden's trickery, he has lost his horse and rides a nag. Beyond the river he beholds an isolated peak and, on the top of it, an extraordinary castle. "Qu'onques si riche forteresce/ Ne virent oil d'ome qui vive" ("So that the eyes of no living man / did see such a rich fortress", vv. 7152-53). From 500 windows as many maidens and ladies show themselves "da la ceinture en de hors" wearing wonderful clothes.

In front of the castle Gauvain hits and smites a knight. He can so take hold of a noble horse and win the ladies' unrestricted admiration.

A boatman meets Gauvain and conveys him the castle ladies' warm invitation. The women ask Yvain for that which is owned to them. He hands over to them the captive knight.

The next morning the boatman discloses to him some unique features of the castle. It lacks both a lord and any knights. It hosts only women and maidens, protected and waited upon by younger or older valets. The defense of the castle relies on mechanical devices. Behind the innumerable windows, automatic or magic bows and crossbows lurk for possible attackers.

The *merveille* of the castle is not restricted to such an amazing defensive system. It features also the mysterious skill of reading men's hearts and detect the vices of the soul:

Que chevalier n'i pot antrer
Qui i poïst mie arester

Demie liue vis ne sains,
Qui fust de covoitise plains
Ne qui ait en lui mal vice
De losainge ne d'avarice.
Coarz ou traïtes n'i dure,
Li foimantie, li parjure,
Cil i muerent si a delivre
Qu'il n'i puent durer ne vivre (vv. 7469-7478).

As no knight can enter it
Or can stay
Alive and healthy, half a league from it,
Who is full of covetousness,
Or hosting any bad vice
Of flattery or greed.
A coward or a traitor don't last there,
The false witness, the perjurer,
They die there so fastly
That they cannot last or survive there.

Actually the castle lies in a waiting condition. The valets cannot become knights. Maiden cannot get married. All the rites of passage which mark the lifecycle are suspended, waiting for the rightful lord to take possession of the castle. Then, the mysterious machines which defend the castle have a selective function: only he who survives all of the dangerous trials will be worthy of ruling the castle.

Gauvain is led by the boatman to a wide entrance. In the main hall a bed embellished by unsurpassed craftsmanship and precious materials stands out in the middle of the main hall. Four wheels allow it to freely flow upon the floor.

Gauvain disregards the boatman's warnings and sits on the Liz de la Merveille. Seven hundred harrows hit his shield and impart him several wounds. Unexpectedly a lion gets out a little room and assaults him.

Gauvain unwaveringly faces and kills the lion. Its paws stays hung unto the shield, one inside and the other outside. Gauvain has passed the test: he is acknowledged as the lord the castle has been expecting for many years. Barrenness has ended. Valets and maidens kneel around him and promise to obey and serve him. The castle resounds with joy, while Gauvain is nourished and dressed in fine robes. The lady of the castle – later identified as Gauvain's grandmother – greets him warmly and news about friends and relatives are gladly exchanged.

The episode of the castle of Chanpguin features an interesting parallel with the previously reviewed segment, as in both instances the uneasy, dangerous access into a closed space lies at the core of the narrative sequence. On the other hand, the two segments features sharply opposing emotional climates. In the Chastel de la Pesme Avventure Yvain had experienced shame, disgrace and dishonour. Gauvain's arrival to the castle of Chanpguin elicits deep joy in the castle ladies, meets the expectations of the whole community and sets the life cycle back in motion.

Obvious differences are apparent also at a plastic and iconic level. Chanpguin Castle enjoys a wonderful location. While Yvain gets into the Chastel de la Pesme Avventure through a little door, entrance to the castle of Chanpguin is wide, the hall is immense.

The Liz de la Merveille features and extraordinary mobility. It flows effortlessly across the wide room. The large, lubricate space stands in opposition to the suffocating, anal atmosphere of the Castel de la Pesme Aventure. Under the volumes of the ladies' castle, we can easily perceive the morphology of the female genital: the pyriform shape, a wide opening, even the diffuse hairiness is paralleled by the countless harrows marking its surface. Freud (1922) did not hesitate to identify a morphologically very similar constellation (Medusa's head covered by snakes) as a typical representative of the female genital. In both the selected episodes from Créthien's romances, the main character is cautioned to surrender, to give up his exploration. There is an obvious conflict between wish and inhibitory forces.

Twin-like relations among peers are pervaded by narcissistic anxieties. Shame is the most conspicuous emotion. On the other hand, in the second text, where the relation with the woman is at issue, the core question is about competence, about the ability to stand up to expectations.

For decades the castle has been waiting for his legitimate lord. Women are in need, they are barren, the little ones cannot grow. Around the ladies by then white-bearded valets busy themselves.

The male principle is longed for, but interaction with the feminine is no easy task: as yet no one has been able to survive the arduous trial. The covetous, the coward, the perjurer are bound to fail. But Gauvain is not frightened, he sits on the Liz de la Merveille. He does not hesitate to unleash the unknown powers of feminine sexuality. He faces the anger, devaluation, loss of control and personal identity which the dynamics of coitus inevitably brings about. He faces the savage lion.

At the end of the mortal combat the ravenous mouth is left between two pawns in the hero's hands: again an extraordinarily iconic representation of the female genital. Joining the female involves sharing the whole span of emotions lying in a female heart – including anger, frustration, powerlessness, devaluation – but the experience is not fruitless. It brings life back to the castle, allows the little ones to grow again. Valets can become knights at last.

Above all, intercourse is a source of happiness in the couple. I am not referring here to concrete bodily pleasures. Maidens and pages bring to Gauvain exquisite food and the finest clothes, but a deeper joy pervades the glad meeting with the ladies of the castle. Those who had been separated since a distant past meet each other again. Family is together again, life appears nicer. Gauvain has been thinking his mother was lost forever, and now discover her as the lady of the castle. He had been able to go beyond childhood only by giving up forever to the warm female embrace. He is an adult now. The sacrifice enforced by the Oedipal taboo is necessary no more. He is now worthy of a woman's love.

The psychoanalytic approach to creative writing has enjoyed variable consensus over the last century. An initial enthusiasm has been followed by increasing dissatisfaction. We have argued here that the often inadequate results brought about by the psychoanalytic reading of literary texts has been due chiefly to a misunderstanding of the peculiar strategies required for drawing full benefits from the identification of partial object unconscious fantasies in texts. In fact, narrative texts of any kind are full with partial objects. This applies to dreams, daydreams, daily life recollections, but even more so to productions of human creativity, including artistic literary texts.

Psychoanalytic readers have been hunting body parts under any kind of manifest narrative, with obvious success. But exposition of symbols in the text offers *per se* no actual advantage for the understanding of the text. We have showed here that partial objects are valuable clues to the deep emotional streams flowing under a manifest text only inasmuch as they are exploited as carriers of emotions. Partial object can elucidate the powerful emotional charge associated with core human object relationships.

In Part II of the present book, we will approach one of the luckiest best seller novel of twenty-first century: *The Da Vinci Code,* by Dan Brown. We will apply to the novel the above reported investigative procedures.

Part II
The Da Vinci Code:
A Pychoanalytic Reading

Popular Literature

In discussing the application of psychoanalytic theory to the understanding of creative writing, Freud expressed the view that psychoanalysis would be particularly useful to understand "die anspruchsloseren Erzähler von Romanen, Novellen und Geschichten, die dafür die zahlreichsten und eifrigsten Leser und Leserinnen finden." ("the more ordinary authors of novels, novellas and short stories, which for this very reason find an innumerable and enthusiastic male and female audience", 1908a, p. 219). Psychoanalysis would then be particularly apt to illuminate the forces which underlie the success of a novel among the general public. The latter would evidently depend on the creative writer's ability to "uns [...] in den Stand setzt, unsere eigenen Phantasien nunmehr ohne Vorwurf und ohne Schämen zu genießen" ("enable us to enjoy now our own fantasies without reproach or shame", *ibidem*, p. 223).

A successful novel should obviously imply themes and interpersonal configurations which are widely shared among men and women who decide to read the book. Under this point of view, a novel selling over 40 millions copies promises to be highly informative. It potentially offers us the code for accessing constellations which are pervasive among humans. This is the code, and no other, we will set out to search for in Dan Brown's masterpiece: *The Da Vinci Code*.

Psychoanalysts has shown a scanty interest in *The Da vinci Code*. In a way it has appeared an easy text, a typical instance of popular culture, somewhat beneath the standards of art creative writing. To the question: "Mais d'où vient le succès du Da Vinci Code?" ("But where does the success of *The Da Vinci Code* come from?") Jacqueline Harpman (2011, p. 36) can find no answer:

ne puis-je rien en sortir que des généralités comme la lutte du bien et du mal,
… la vœu inconscient de recevoir un déchiffrement de ces secrets que l'on se
fait à soi-même, ou, encore plus banal, la quête des secrets de la scène
primitive (*ibidem*, p. 37).

> I can find nothing more than generic issues, such as the struggle between the Good and the Evil, [...] the unconscious wish to get a decoding of those secrets which one creates for himself, or, even more trite, the search for the secrets of the primal scene.

More consistently with Freud's interest in popular novels, Mariam Cohen (2004) devoted to *The Da Vinci Code* a scientifically accurate psychoanalytic study. Cohen acknowledges Dan Brown's full mastery of the techniques which are specific to thriller writing, but believes the novel success is based on a deeper level fantasy content. In Cohen's view, a psychodynamic de-coding of the text would unveil a universal, regressive unconscious phantasm. She writes: "The benign sort of conspiracy that Brown's Priory of Sion represents is this sort of womb that all of us may harbour some deeply unconscious wish to return to" (Cohen, 2004, p. 737). The struggle between Langdom and the wicked conspirator Leigh Teabing could then be traced back to the little male child's fantasy of enjoying mother's unlimited love and seize father's power. Over the narrative the main character, and implicitly the regressing reader, would prevail over Oedipal competitors and "wins an adult sexual status" (p. 739).

Cohen's work undoubtedly offers interesting hints on the unconscious contents of Brown's highly successful novel. We have however to point out that unconscious fantasies Cohen detected in the narrative material are extremely pervasive among humans. As such they can be detected in most or all similar novels.

In *Der Dichter un das Phantasieren* Freud (1908a) mentioned narcissistic wishes of power and success beside erotic wishes as prototypical components of commercial novel narratives. Fear of and wish for control and availability of omnipotent parents' imagos characterise conspiracy novels as a literary genre rather than *The Da Vinci Code* as a specific creative text.

I think a psychoanalytic reading of a literary work can really be heuristically rewarding only inasmuch as it can go beyond generic themes and proves able to unveil text-specific unconscious contents. To that aim a generic reliance on some narrative component of the plot should be deemed insufficient. A methodologically accurate psychoanalytic approach to a literary text should be able to offer evidence of a sequence of biunivocal correspondences between the inferred unconscious narrative and the manifest text. This microscopy level interpretative task need be carried out on limited and specified text segments. In the following we will show the reader how this interpretative approach can unveil under Dan Brown's thriller novel a much more complex network of unconscious patterns than previously hypothesized.

Chapter Four
A Deeper Code

Dan Brown's novel tells a story about a code. The second main character – Sophie Neveu – is a professional cryptologist, listed in the ranks of French Police. Actually, the interpretation of an elusive code is the very focus of Langdom's and Sophie Neveu's painstaking efforts. Enigmas are presented and resolved one after the other all through the novel.

Enigmas are devised in order to protect secrets. They warrant sensitive information is withdrawn from hostile or however unsuited listeners, readers, watchers. Enigmas are also means for communicating information to friendly or more adequately trained individuals. As a vehicle of restricted information, as a communicative medium to a selected audience, enigmas are quintessential to the needs and operations of secret societies and of initiatory cults of any kind since antiquity. This undoubtedly lends enigmas a prominent status within *The Da Vinci Code*, a novel about a secret, initiatory, mystery society.

From our psychoanalytic point of view, however, enigmas are clearly vital to the needs and functions of unconscious communication. Repression is the core device human relies on in order to protect anxiety-provoking information from undue leaks.

While working on the traumatic experiences of hysterical patients, Freud (1895, p. 89) discovered the functioning of the human mind is so articulated as to restrain access to potentially dangerous pieces of information. Through repression anxiety provoking materials are withdrawn from both the subject's awareness and other individuals' unwanted attention.

However, the function of repression in human mind wouldn't be sufficiently characterised in terms of mere withdrawal of information. Repression both withdraws it and conveys it. Through dreams, parapraxes, through the patient's free associations in the analytic hour – no less than through creative writing – anxiety provoking, upsetting information is transmitted in a disguised form to potential listeners, to listeners in some way trained to the rules of unconscious communication. This double, apparently contradictory function clearly establishes a parallel between repression and purposely formulated enigmas. Freud (1900, p. 267 ff.) himself posed the fate of Oedipus, solver of the enigma of the Sphinx, as the very core metaphor of the psychoanalytic endeavour.

The Da Vinci Code revolves around a multi-letter code. The code would allow the interpreter to find out Mary Magdalene's bones. However, if we lend adequate attention to the novel core words, we rapidly realize encoded material is much more widely spread over the text. My attention was particularly elicited by the characters' names. Some of them are commonly used in the country the corresponding character is said to come from. Others are pretty unusual.

However a trained cryptographer is certainly not required in order to realize that nearly all characters' names in the novel are amenable to be transformed in object names through simple letter exchanges or inversions. Through anagrams and analogous letter combinatory operations *The Da Vinci Code* characters' names disclose an occult system of meanings, mainly alluding to specific body parts or functions.

An interpretative grid summarizing this thick network of phonetic and semantic clues is offered to the reader in the tables at the end of the present chapter. In the left column the main characters' names are listed. Each of them is assumed to disguise a different but somewhat cognate name (Column 3), referring to bodily parts or functions, these in turn listed in Column 4. In the last column phonetic and semantic evidence is offered in support of the tentative interpretations.

Just as the novel manifest content, the latent one alludes to an occult meaning. No ancient brotherhood, though, watches upon this enigma. Rather the mental operations which the human unconscious typically relies on: the mechanisms which Freud discovered while studying the process of dream formation (1900, Ch. VI), which amount to the various strategies through which repression withdraws upsetting mental contents from awareness.

The Da Vinci Code appears to be encoded. Inasmuch as a human creative text, the novel is encrypted in the specific coded language of the unconscious mind. Its disguised contents can therefore be retrieved only through a specific technical operation: interpretation.

We cannot obviously review here the procedures and strategies the analyst's mind relies on in order to reach a comprehensive and reliable interpretation of a manifest mental content. However, the patient's reaction to an interpretation undoubtedly amounts to a core criteria for assessing the validity of an expressive intervention. Resolution or change of a symptom, changes in the quality of the therapeutic situation in terms of alliance, transference or characteristics of association flows, emerging of new material: all of the above may be evidence that an interpretative act has hit or at least approached significant unconscious contents.

Applied psychoanalysis obviously lacks this confirmatory opportunity. The textual code we are here analysing cannot respond to our interventions. Our interpretative efforts may rather be tested in terms of the internal consistency of the reconstruction of the unconscious narrative they may allow to outline. For our specific task here, useful and reliable interpretations of the characters' names will be those which will enable us to formulate an articulated and consistent understanding of the unconscious fantasies underlying the *Da Vinci Code* text.

The Decoding Grid - I				
Character's name	Role in the novel	Cognate, disguised name	Related body part	Relevant evidence
Robert Langdom	The main character. A symbologist	LONG + CONDOM	Penis	A body part whose length increases preliminary to intercourse and is exquisitely associated to Oedipal anxieties.
Sophie Neveu	Langdom's associate. A Cryptologist	SOFFIO DI NEVE, Italian for BLOW OF SNOW, leading to the opposite: STINKING BREATH	Petum	The name SOPHIE stems from the Greek word for wisdom. Phonetically it associates closely with the Italian word SOFFIO (French SOUFFLE, English BREATH). NEVEU is the French word for NEPHEW, but also an obsolete synonymous with GRANDSON/GRANDDAUGHTER, *i.e.,* Neveu's specific family relation to Curator Saunier. However, phonetically, it associates closely to the Italian NEVE (SNOW). Snow is white, it is synonymous with beauty and cleanliness. However, in the human body gas are often stinky and may also be ejected through the anus. In as far as faeces constitute the very paradigm of dirtiness, the opposition to the qualities of snow couldn't be more extreme. The use of reaction formation can be considered very likely here.

The Decoding Grid - II

Character's name	Role in the novel	Cognate, disguised name	Related body part	Relevant evidence
Bezu Fache	A police officer. Langdom 's main antagonist	FACE OF CHIN, FACCIA DI CAZZO, Italian for PENIS FACE	The objectual penis	Bezu is phonetically cognate of BAZZA, an obsolete and highly literary Italian word for chin. Parallels from folklore may show how chin may include phallic hints. In *König Drosselbart* – a folk tale which is widespread over Europe and is included in Brothers Grim's collection (KHM 52) – the main character features an unusually conspicuous chin. Its length elicits a particularly intense distaste in the young female character. The Italian version of the tale is titled *Re Bazza di Tordo.* A parallel line of thought may lead us to the phonetically cognate French word BAISE which is a standard euphemisms for sexual intercourse. FACHE is the French word for FACE; if we admit BEZU may allude to the male gentital we may decode BEZU FACHE as FACCIA DI CAZZO (penis face) perhaps the most common abusive epithet in Italian everyday speech.

The Decoding Grid - III

Character's name	Role in the novel	Cognate, disguised name	Related body part	Relevant evidence
Jacques Sauniere	The Curator of the Louvre Museum *and* the leader of the Priory of Sion. He is the victim of the murder setting the narrative in motion	SONNEUR, French for MUSIC PLAYER.	Objectual anus	The word SAUNIERE is phonetically cognate with the French *SONNEUR*, *i.e.,* MUSIC PLAYER. It implies an allusion to a body part which expels gases and produces sounds. The association with sound is apparent also in the curator's Christian name: JACQUES. In the most widely spread tune in the world, *Frère Jacques*, bell playing is the friar's main task. Also the term Curator, describing Sauniere position as the head of the Musée du Louvre may involve resonances with the latin CULUS.
Silas	The murderer	LISA, MONNA LISA, FLEUR DA LYS	Male generativity within an ambiguous sexual identity	The fanatic Catholic killer's name may be anagrammed into LISA. The relationship with Leonardo's masterpiece MONNA LISA – incidentally on display at the Louvre Museum – need not be further illuminated. The FLEUR DA LYS, the heraldic representative of lilium, is closely associated with French kingship and is the emblem of the enigmatic priory of Sion. Lilium shows a uniquely erected attitude, is a symbol of fertility since antiquity and is particularly associated with the Annunciation to Mother Mary

The Decoding Grid - IV

Character's name	Role in the novel	Cognate, disguised name	Related body part	Relevant evidence
Aringarosa	Prelate of the Opus Dei. Only late in the novel we realize he only unwittingly has fostered Prof. Teabing's criminal projects.	ARINGA ROSA, Italian for PINK HERRING	Little (childish) penis	The family name Aringarosa may easily be split in two Italian words: ARINGA (HERRING) and ROSA (PINK). Fish is a universal euphemism for the male (and sometimes female) genital. The association is reinforced by the mention of the western men's skin colour. The choice of a very small fish may be a reference to an early stage of the life-cycle or however to feelings of helplessness when confronted with adult males.
Leigh Teabing	The occult puppeteer setting out the network of lies and murders. In a word: the culprit.	BINGE EATING	Mouth	LEIGH TEABING is a partial anagram of BINGE EATING. The latter is a medical term and refers to discrete episodes of uncontrolled food consumption which is observed in a few eating disorders. Requirement for the access to Teabing's mansion is the ability to answer a specific question about tastes. The association with alimentary behaviour seems to support a connection with the oral area.

The Decoding Grid - V

Character's name	Role in the novel	Cognate, disguised name	Related body part	Relevant evidence
Remi Legaleduc	Personal servant and driver to Prof. Teabing	(DO)-RE-MI + LÉCHAGE DE CUL: French for a LICK OF THE ASS	Oro-anal intercourse.	Mr. Legaleduc's name includes an allusion to sound production, the notes RE and MI (D and E in the Anglo-Germanic notation system). By adding the first step in the C scale we have the first segment of the melody of Frère Jacques (again!), the most universally known melody in western civilization. Taken together, this train of association seems to imply an amount of overlap or parallel with the symbolic function of the previously discussed name of Jacques Sauniere, which also includes allusions to the anal sphincter. Such hints are reinforced and made clearer by Remy's family name: LEGALEDUC. A slightly altered anagram of Legaleduc is the French LECHAGE DE CUL (LICK OF THE ASS) and also the Italian LECCACULO. In Italy this is the most frequent word of abuse in commenting organizational behaviour. In facts, besides alluding to a specific sexual practice, LECACCULO is a common metaphor for an attitude of absolutely proness towards people in power. In essence, linguistical and phonetical clues support the hypothesis the name REMY LEGALEDUC is associated both to a body area (the anus) and to a to a specific form of oral sexual gratification in which the contact with and the slavish care of the object's body is highly invested and eroticised.

The Decoding Grid - VI

Character's name	Role in the novel	Cognate, disguised name	Related body part	Relevant evidence
Marie Chauvel	Sophie Neveu's grandmother	MARIE + CHEVAUX (French for HORSES) and CHEVEUX (French for HAIR)	Protective, generative Penis	Marie's surname is a nearly exact anagram of CHEVAUX, plural of the French word for HORSE; and also of CHEVEUX, French word for HAIR . Here the male genital implied by the allusion to the horse is morphologically associated with a surprisingly long white hair. A representation of the male pubic area may reinforce the onomastic associations. On the other hand, MARIE, the name of the Mother of God, elicits memories of childhood and maternal care. Any allusion to aggression and threat is so excluded from the semantic field.

Chapter Five
**Selection and Exploration
of the Unconscious Narratives**

NARRATIVE MATERIAL SELECTED FOR THE ANALYSIS

Dream thoughts rely on narratives as their main communicative device. In order to get access to dream thoughts underlying a literary text we have to preliminarily identify meaningful narrative sequences within the text. Obviously, due to the multidetermination of any product of the unconscious mind, selected narratives will shown various degree of overlapping at a manifest content level.

Our analysis will rely on the following narrative segments:

A. THE GENERAL PLOT

Robert Langdom, the main character, is blamed with a murder, the victim being Jacques Saunier, the old and respected Curator of the Louvre Museum. On a phone call by the police, the cryptologist Robert Langdom is summoned to the crime scene. He penetrates the Grand Galerie where the Curator has fallen. The criminal police officer Captain Bezu Fache believes he is the perpetrator of the crime. Robert Langdom meets Miss Sophie Neveu, the victim's granddaughter. From then on, they will flee together, followed by Bezu Fache's men in a breathtaking manhunt, which will end in Scotland.

B. SOPHIE NEVEU'S STORY.

It is a girl's story. Sophie is orphaned in her early infancy. Mother and father dies in a mysterious car crash. Her grandfather, the murderer's victim, is all is left to her, and affectionately cares for her for a long time. Sophie's discovery of a secret liturgical assembly where he is performing sex rituals on a masked woman permanently spoils their relations. At the end of the story she meets her grandmother again after decades.

C. AN INSTITUTIONAL-GROUP LEVEL NARRATIVE.

Two powerful organizations face each other in the novel: the Catholic Church – with *Opus Dei* as its front line, elite troops – and an enigmatic secret society, the Priory of Sion. Both institutions are real, but in the course of the novel their representations undergo a radical transformation. In the end we are acutely surprised to know that the deadly challenge between the Catholic Church and the Priory of Sion has been a pure mystification, the tragic charade of a savage anticlerical: Prof. Leigh Teabing

DECODING THE MAIN PLOT.

Level of Analysis.

The main plot entails many features which are suggestive of a part object narrative level:

a. As shown in the above reported Decoding Grid an even superficial review of main plot characters' names shows an astonishing quality. Practically all of them may be transformed through simple combinatory procedures into words alluding to body parts or functions.

b. In the main plot narratives an unusual attention is lent to characters' movements within the physical-geometrical space:

    b.1 Langdom has to crawl under a grate in order to enter the Grand Galerie wing and inspect the crime scene. He moves along the aisle, then penetrate the toilet and is believed to have leapt from a window.

    b.2 He endures the uneasy trial of crossing UBS caveau gates.

    b.3 He needs again some wit to induce Teabing to allow him access to Château Villette.

    b.4 His and Leigh Teabing's movements into the Templar Chapel and later the Westminster abbey receive enhanced attention.

    c.   Most main plot characters display morphological peculiarities that invite to a parallel with specific body parts. Bezu Fache shows a vintage hair style with a sharp widow peak and a stout appearance. Sophie Neveu shifts objects into and out of a pocket included in her ever present sweater. Sophie's grandma displays a long white hair which is at odd with her age and role in the life cycle.

The General Narrative Frame: the Runaway.

The Da Vinci Code narrative is dominated by a hasty flight. Robert Langdom flees from French police and from a dangerous organization whose agent is ruthlessly willing to kill again in order to seize a secret Langdom is assumed to possess.

We have reported above evidence suggesting this textual level is organized in terms of an interaction between partial objects. Actually, narrative sequences gain consistency if we conceptualize them as interactions between body parts rather than between individuals. We may reformulate the main characters in terms of partial object representatives as follows:

A. THE ANGRY OX

At the level of the explicit narrative Robert Langdom flees from a man: the powerful and determinate Captain Bezu Fache. His personality features clearly allude to conventional male prowess. This calls our attention towards the area of male sexualised body. Other clues may help refine our search. Bezu Fache appearance is described in some detail:

> Captain Bezu Fache carried himself like an angry ox, with his wide shoulders thrown back and his chin tucked hard into his chest. His dark hair was slicked back with oil, accentuating an arrow-like widow's peak that divided his jutting brow and preceded him like the prow of a battleship (p. 23).

A couple of features in Fache's complexion may be worth of our attention: a) a neck is hardly perceivable joining his head and trunk, and b) his peculiar hairdress draws a longitudinal mark across the vertex of his head.

These two details establish an obvious parallel with the plastic shape of the male genital. The penis, too, appears as made up by two volumes (*asta* and *glande*) adjoined without an apparent caesura. And the urethral meatus definitely cuts its vertex longitudinally.

The parallel with the male genital is further supported by the name of the captain of Direction de Policie Judiciare (DPJ). In fact, the analysis reported in our Decoding Grid shows the words BEZU FACHE suggest an identification of the head or rather the full body with a phallus (an identification which has long been known to psychoanalytic literature; *cfr.* Freud 1900, pp. 370-371; Lewin, 1933).

B. AN INSEPARABLE COUPLE

Langdom flees for most of the book. But he is not fleeing alone. A female cryptologist is *always* with him. To the aim of the present investigation this constant association advocates for a joint treatment of the two characters. The main plot is highly liable to a partial object level interpretation. Within this framework the main character couple may fruitfully be interpreted in terms of different, but in a way complementary body parts.

The Decoding Grid offers us intriguing evidence from such perspective. Specifically, the Decoding Grid shows us Prof. Langdom's name implies associations to the sexually activated male genital. On the other hand, for Sophie Neveau, semantic evidence seems to warrant an association with the anal sphincter. This line of interpretation leads us to admit that the persistent association of Neveu with Langdom thrives on an *anatomical* basis. In the main plot the two characters serve the function of plastically representing two core components of perineal area in males: the penis and the anus.

The identification of the representational value of the three main characters in the novel allows us now to formulate the unconscious narrative underlying the novel main plot in a deeper and more intriguing way. The perineal area features an extraordinary reactivity to tactile stimulation. Willingness to expose to others, to a bodily interaction with others, such vulnerable area means trusting them the power to heavily affect our level of arousal. Exposure to others' sight or manipulation of our own penis and anus has an enormous social and personal significance. Whenever this occurs outside the most close and intimate relationships, embarrassment, rage, excitation, and fear are elicited. Male and female prostitution gives a sad proof that the access to others' perineal area may possess an enormous both subjective and objective value.

Control of the access to our intimacy is a vital component of human interpersonal behaviour. For most individuals the enforcement of a restricted access to intimacy heavily affects the articulation of core object relations, including the establishment of both couple life and intergenerational barriers. In fact, Donald Meltzer (1973, p. 84) has brilliantly demonstrated how the primal scene fantasy may be conceived as a basic representation and a paradigm of the multiple wishes and fears, pleasures and pains associated with different roles in the human couple and family.

From the perspective of our present investigation, the dimension of fear (of being penetrated, invaded, controlled by others) may prove particularly illuminating. *The Da Vinci Code* main plot narrative depicts a flight: desperate, relentless, convulse. It is the flight of a male representative – a male and a woman characters as representative of male intimacy – from a threat, a male dominating threat.

The emotion associated to this flight is spelled out plainly: it is fear. At the start of the novel Langdom fears to be arrested and receive a life sentence. Later on, he and Sophie fear to be killed by Silas, as other novel characters have been earlier in the narrative. In the last pages Leigh Teabing threatens to shot them personally with an handgun. Robert Langdom's is the ultimate fear, then: fear of death.

Criptex Associated Narratives

Blindness

Alone in the darkness,
My sight opaque,
I stagger about
On the verge of chaos.

Suddenly,
Deep under the sea,
High among the steepest cliffs,
At the core of unquenchable blazes,
I stumble into the Secret Casket.

The code do I break
And you can I see,

My truth, my love.

Secondary Characters and a Featured Item.

Main plot events extends over a restricted time span: forty-eight hours. However, the main narrative is highly articulated. It incorporates a number of lower-order narrative segments, which are staged by ancillary characters.

Some of these interactions are complex and involve a focus on the movement of volumes within the space. Actually much of the narrative revolves around the possess of an inanimate object, the Criptex. We have shown above how these features may give evidence that a narrative episode includes partial object level material.

In the next section we will then discuss a possible interpretation of the unconscious meanings associated with the following characters and an item:

    a. Silas the killer and bishop Aringarosa.
    b. The treacherous ally, Leigh Teabing.
    c. An unusual container: the Cryptex.

A. THE KILLER AND HIS MENTOR: SILAS AND ARINGAROSA

As reported above, *The Da Vinci Code* is the story of a flight. Robert Langdom flees dangerous criminals' hunter Bezu Fache. At the same time, he is the coveted game in a much more dangerous hunt. Silas, the impassible, goal driven, frighteningly determined, outwardly redeemed criminal, is out at him.

Silas knows no faltering when bound to kill. In the novel he kills 5 times. He shoots Jacques Sauniere, the Curator of the Louvre Museum, so setting the narrative machinery in motion. He kills poor nun Sandrine in the hope of seizing the mysterious *keystone.* We learn that he has previously killed the three Senechaux of the Priory of Sion. In fact he is fully determined to kill anyone opposing his ultimate task, the retrieval of the keystone. This makes Robert Langdom the most likely next target for his never missing handgun.

Robert Langdom flees the police. Police chase Langdom as DPJ officers believe Langdom is guilty of murder. Since the first pages of the novel we know, though, that Langdom is innocent. He is wanted for a crime another has committed.

He risks paying the penalty of Silas' deeds. This establishes a peculiar and intriguing connection between the two characters. And invites us to explore to a deeper extent their relationship at a partial object level.

Our decoding grid supports partial object associations for Silas' no less than Langdom's name. In addition, Silas' appearance is unique. He is described as an albino: his skin is depigmented. He is white, bald, his disquieting reddish eyes spotting the centre of his face. His dress is unique, too. As a numerary member of Opus Dei, he wears a robe with a hood. His somatic and general appearance shows a striking parallel with that of the manly member: slightly curved, the junction between the corpus and the glans marked by an indented collar. And with a reddish opening at the vertex. The cap also may allude to the movable quality of the preputius, which in turn elicits association with the physiology of male sexuality.

Silas operates alone on the field. However, his personality features are highly stylised. His strategies and choices can be understood only in light of his relations to a powerful religious institution: the *Opus Dei.* To be more specific, Silas' personal history as well as his role in the novel get full consistency and meaning only against the background of his close and faithful relationship to Opus Dei fictitious *Prelate,* bishop Aringarosa. Silas is said to owe everything –

life, freedom and, more deeply, any sense of meaning in life – to his master's unquestionable long term and unwavering availability.

As mentioned in the Grid, Aringarosa's name includes an array of allusions to the male genital. However implied features differ, rather oppose those apparent in the plastic representation of the albino killer. They include references to the colour of human skin and to a very little fish. They seem to evoke images of male infancy. They suggest weakness, frailty.

Aringarosa is a member of the Catholic clergy, he's a traditionalist clergyman. We therefore expect him to wear a cassock, i.e. a female–like dress. Silas and Aringarosa constitute in the novel a peculiar composite. Dependence, passivity, weakness imply the giving up of a male, phallic identity. The pale Silas, on the other hand, elicits associations with a dangerous, potentially lethal phallus.

Silas' and Aringarosa's goals and motives in the relationship with the other characters are as much bifront. For most of the novel we are led to believe that the two of them are weaving an obscure and murderous web around the other characters. The end of the novel will cast a completely different light on this couple and its motives.

For the time being we must point out that for several hundred pages to Langdom and the reader Silas appears as a callous and determinate killer. We learn he has killed 5 people and has made up his mind to dispose of Prof. Langdom, and possibly Sophie Neveu, and to take hold of their precious Criptex. At a partial object level the danger of being killed by Silas, a character depicting and representing a phallus, may be revelatory of an enhanced fear of being aggressively penetrated. Of being the victim of a powerful attack, including intense sadistic and inhuman components.

B. THE JANUS-FACED HISTORIAN

Leigh Teabing plays a unique role in the plot machinery. Brown introduces him to us as a valuable partner in the struggle between Langdon and his pursuers. He proves later to be a traitor: the occult puppeteer staging the deceitful narrative unfolding in front of the other characters' eyes, as well as plotting their early death.

Greed is the most striking feature in Teabing's character. He covets Langdom owned cryptex, the mysterious keystone, with unwavering determination. He ruthlessly wastes several human lives to the aim of possessing the object which would allow him to settle down once and forever his lifetime struggle against the Catholic Church.

Plastic details in Teabing's description offered by the novel further attract our attention on the oral motivation domain. A leg of his is supported by a metal tutor device. Due to the advancement of dentistry, for many of us, the integrity of dental apparatus is maintained through bridges, implant fixtures and other metal devices. The character's name further supports an association with the oral cavity. Our Decoding Grid indicates Teabing's name includes specific allusions to oral wishes. As regards the manifest object of such wishes the novel is unambiguous: the enigmatic Cryptex.

C. THE CRYPTEX

The investment of all of the characters in the Renaissance style, highly secretive envelope is in itself strongly suggestive of a partial object function within the unconscious phantasy underlying the main plot of *The Da Vinci Code*. The anatomical correlation with the male genital is supported by a number of plastic and functional features. The cryptex is cylindrical. It can be opened, like the vertex of a penis, when erected.

Inside it a white liquid is hidden. We learn it can be shed and that this represents a great risk. His surface is wooden: it is hard, but the map inside it is made of leather, a material obviously associated with living beings.

Unfolding the Criptex Narratives

The carefully hidden treasure of the Priory of Sion, the goal of all of Langdom's efforts for a long section of *The Da Vinci Code*, the ominous, murderous Teacher's libidinal object, the *clef de voûte*, the secret key which gives access to the most carefully guarded secret in the history of mankind, implicitly the key to final knowledge and peace: the Criptex is all of this – and even more. As we have shown above, within unconscious symbolism, it is a representation of the penis.

The cryptex is an object of wishes, intense wishes. The Priory of Sion Senecheux – and now Langdom as the implicit heir of the Priory ideals and goals – are ready to give up their life to the aim of protecting it. Teabing actually wastes the life of a number of people to the aim of seizing it.

In *The Da Vinci Code* manifest content characters' motives are explicitly focused on the Grail, here identified with a woman's bones. Actually, in the thrilling plot, which keeps the reader permanently anxious for the fate of Robert Langdom, the Grail is never actually present. Struggle always revolves around the Cryptex.

Three narrative segments share this specific dramatic feature: at the Château Villette, Teabing's gorgeous estate; at the Temple Church, where the last Temple leaders lie buried; and in the resolutory confrontation at Saint Paul's Cathedral. These scenes are played out by a somewhat standardised set of characters: Langdom, Teabing and Neveu always attend. At Chateu Villlette and and at Temple Church Silas is also present. He does not participate in the last act of the struggle for the cryptex at Saint Paul's Cathedral. Dan Brown's creativity is however able to compose a parallel narrative which concurrently unfolds in front of the readers' eyes. Silas' life is at stake – and finally lost – the very moment Langdom and Teabing confront each other at the two ends of a small revolver.

The repetitive quality of such narratives allows the extraction of a shared pattern. In all three these cryptex related episodes:

a. Life is in immediate danger: Langdom's and implicitly the reader's, inasmuch as identificatory processes are implicit in any reading experience.
b. Handguns are on the scene. Their phallic symbolic power is traditionally admitted. We do not need discussing it any longer.
c. The characters confronting each other in the episodes struggle for a specific object: the Cryptex. Langdom do not hesitate to risk his life in order to keep control of it.
d. Cryptex related risk is two-fold: a) of losing control of it and b) of letting it break, i.e. letting its content spill away.
d. Against such framework Silas' presence yields a deeper, more ominous fear. He's got used to kill. His determination is blind. He knows not Sir Teabing's complex strategies, he's an immediate and murderous machine.

I believe data summarized here offer adequate evidence for formulating the unconscious phantasy underlying the three relationship episodes. As was the case for the main plot, cryptex related episodes possess an unmistakable partial object quality. We have previously discussed the partial object associations implied by the three characters involved: Langdom, Sophie Neveu and Teabing clearly allude to the male genital, anal and oral areas. The cryptex shows both morphological and functional analogies with the penis. We have commented also on pale Silas's features representing an erected ominous male member.

Further evidence of a partial object narrative structure comes from the characters' movements in such episodes. Most or all attention stays focused on the characters' changing position in space, on their stepping and falling, as well as on the vertical movements of the Cryptex. As a general rule, abundant partial object material call our attention to a highly invested unconscious constellation: an eroticized semantic field, where wishes reach an extreme intensity and find no predictable satisfaction, inasmuch as it is fully dependent on the object's hoped for compliance.

Among the episode characters, no allusion could we find to the female genital. The internal coitus phantasy we are here exposed to does not involve the two opposite sexes. No allusion is made to a marital embrace. Responsibility for the generation of children is not at issue.

The intense anxiety is rather rooted in an identity conflict. The representation of phallus is doubled. On the field the ominous and savage penis-like albino is confronted with a team of characters whose connections to male anatomy we have discussed already. Langdom and Neveu represent the male vulnerability, the hazards implicit in passivity.

In relationships between equals, narcissistic adjustments come to be extremely fragile. In the interacting couple no factual polarities are discernible. The balance in a twin-like couple is prone to suddenly and unpredictably swing into a confrontation between competitors.

Twin births are believed to be particularly ominous in various primitive cultures (Girard, 1972, p. 88-92). To settle the issue many primitive tribes kill one or both members of any twin couple. The most primitive fear elicited by the Oedipal triangulation would appear to be that of being substituted *tout-court* in the relationship to the mother by a peer.

The opposition between activity and passivity is particularly suitable to represent and sort hierarchically informed interactions: strong/weak, big/small, elder/younger. Within this framework the polar qualities which are apparent in the heterogeneous couple Aringarosa/Silas come to be less elusive. Male eroticized friendship may thrive on a submissive attitude, on an explicit willingness to give up phallic ambitions to the advantage of a child-like compliance with the object's wishes. Savage Silas may well give way to meek Aringarosa. But balance is highly unstable. The dangers of an enacted, sadistically charged Oedipus, the threat from an omnipotent, controlling, devouring father, may rapidly resurface in the unconscious mind whenever the partners in a highly invested interaction are equals, are ὁμοῖος, *i.e.,* are homosexual.

Plastic Scenario

Collected data allow us to better formulate narrative sequences underlying cryptex-related episodes. We are now assuming each of those three episodes disguise a sexual interaction between same sex subjects: between two males.

Greed enhances tension: oral-featured Teabing longs for the Cryptex/penis. Langdom's friendly manipulation of the Cryptex isn't enough. Teabing strives for the possession, the incorporation of the male token. Danger peaks. Sophie Neveu is at least twice in immediate danger of being shot.

As shown in the grid, associations to the latter character's name implies that anal penetration is at issue. The narrative sequence lets us perceive a dismaying threat. Death is at hand: main characters' individual death, Priory of Sion members' collective death, and the ultimate death of any human hope for freedom and truth.

A somatic solution is as much at hand. The at length threatened crumbling of the Cryptex for a moment appears to be the only way out. The premature shedding of the milky, sour liquid has the power to put the male sexual apparatus at rest, producing a refractory period. The male motivational and motor forces may so withdraw from the object. Peace comes. Silas' flight gets to its end and he droops on a bench: intercourse ceases.

Emotional Scenario

We have mentioned above how *The Da Vinci Code* main plot is plainly dominated by fear. We may see how here Langdom's life is endangered by male strength, authority, and father-like, superegoic forces. Threat is male here. But the victims in the narrative share obvious correlates of male identity, though articulated in a more complex representation. Langdom and Sophie: penis and anus. The bold, prow and the week, sensitive sides of male body and identity. Maleness: whenever primal scene material surfaces in the main plot it features an homosexual, a male and homosexual quality.

In *The Da Vinci Code,* primal scene lacks a womb: no vagina, no womb, no container function in Bion's sense (1962, pp. 90 ff.). The wish to penetrate and control the object from within, to alleviate fears of homelessness and rejection by the mother object can meet no compliance. Here, aggression cannot be redeemed by maternal love.

Interaction is close. And hot. Langdom and Silas are determined, but their goals are too similar. Teabing's immoderate greed to seductively control the male object is on the verge of success. Control of the Cryptex seems at hand. Langdom is frightened, though, as Sophie is at stake:

> Sophie Neveu sensed him too late. Before she could turn, Silas pressed the gun barrel into her spine and wrapped a powerful arm across her chest, pulling her back against his hulking body. She yelled in surprise (p. 362).

In the primal scene fantasy underlying *The Da Vinci Code* narrative, object relation qualities coalesces around two poles: at the one end we find strength, power, control, at the opposite end we find fear, dependence, helplessness. Positions within the internal coitus seem here to definitely assign roles, better full identities along this axis: on the one side the self-assured, dominating and judging father, on the other the weak, dependent, helpless child. The latter identification is associated in this fantasy with intense fears. Being penetrated, being invaded, being dominated are here frightening experiences. Life, emotional life, and core identity are at stake.

Main Plot: a Synthesis

In front of us a rich material is lying. The novel main plot has been solved into its elementary components. Its partial objects underpinnings have been largely illuminated. The novel narrative has given proof to revolve mainly around the issue of a relationship between equals, within a twin-like symmetric couple: between subjects sharing a common male anatomy.

In *The Da Vinci Code*, a phantasmal unintentional homosexual contact is associated with an excruciating dilemma, a dynamic conflict. Subjective greed is intense. Ability to elicit sexual excitement involves a control over the interacting object.

Power is so alluring. A sound, meek Aringarosa can be turned into a blind, dumb Silas, the unaware slave of hidden powers. The possess of the Criptex could yield an unlimited power, but greed is blind. Greed exposes Teabing to the risk of losing everything. It exposes Langdom to the risk of losing what appears in the novel to be most valuable to him: Sophie.

Seduction yields power, but involves permeability. Involves passive availability to the object's projections. Somatic penetration reflects actual emotional reality inasmuch as it implies and represents the active insertion of unconscious contents into the object's Self.

The feared, implicitly sadistic, quality of homosexual penetration alludes to the aggressive violent insertion of unpleasant, faecal mental contents into the object, it alludes to the malignant form of projective identification which was described by Melanie Klein in her well know paper on schizoid mechanisms (1946, p. 8). Intimacy involves vulnerability. Unrestricted contact may well offer power over the excited object, but the naked body is permeable, lies in permanent danger.

The Da Vinci Code main plot talks us about this struggle. The abolition of boundaries in front of the male object traps the subject between the allure of power and the fear of external aggressive control. Langdom is able to escape Silas' and Teabing's chase in the end. Only later on, having trailed some more into the book, will we be able to grasp the emotional constellation allowing the narrating subject to eventually escape this dismaying emotional aporia.

A DECEASED FAMILY

The Da Vinci Code chronicles a two-days hunt to Langdom and his Cryptex. The report of chase-related events, however, is intertwined with a few older stories: the 2000 year long history of mainstream Christianity and of the somewhat concurrent religious tradition handed down from generation to generation within the esoteric brotherhood of the Priory of Sion; and also a shorter, in a way more private, story. That of a murdered family.

In Chapter 13 the author informs us that Sophie Neveu, the extremely clever French cryptologist, and Curator Sauniere, the first victim of Sila's malicious deeds, share one and the same blood: they are grandfather and granddaughter. Later on, prompted by Langdom's questioning, Sophie opens up a box of sad memories. We readers come then to know the tragedy of Sophie's family.

Dan Brown lends Sophie's report a distinctively controlled emotional quality. She plainly and directly tells Langdom how both her parents, her grandmother and her little brother have died in a car accident. Sophie adds then that the facts of life have been able to fully alienate her from her only surviving relationship, grandfather Sauniere.

Over the course of the novel Langdom reaches the goal of his quest. He finds the Grail. Sophie Neveu meets with an as much or personally even worthier accomplishment. She finds again her living relatives and reconciles herself with the dead ones. She discovers her grandmother and younger brother are still alive and meets them next to Rosslyn Chapel, Scotland.

Neveu's narratives extends between sharply opposing poles. The image of a child losing her parents, her full family, is apt to elicit the most intense sympathetic emotional pain. A reader can very hardly resist to resonate with the most basic fear each of us has experienced in early infancy. Nor could I stay indifferent to the wave of life and well-being radiating from the little hut bordering Rosslyn premises:

> Out on the bluff, the fieldstone house was exactly as Sophie remembered it. Night was falling now, and the house exuded a warm and inviting aura. The smell of bread wafted through the opened screened door, and a golden light shone in the windows [...]
>
> An eternity seemed to pass as the two women stared at one another through the thin mesh. Then, like the slowly gathering swell of an ocean wave, the woman's visage transformed from one of uncertainty... to disbelief... to hope... and finally, to cresting joy.
>
> Throwing open the door, she came out, reaching with soft hands, cradling Sophie's thunderstruck face. "Oh, dear child... look at you!" (p. 440-441).

Sophie and Marie find each other at last, each of them trusting life again, each of them able again to fully rely on the others as a persistent source of nurturance and warmth. Sophie's narrative in *The Da Vinci Code* gives wide evidence of intense splitting processes: darkness and light, bereavement and meeting again with relatives, desperate loneliness and family warmth follow each other abruptly and unexpectedly. Between these internally consistent absolutes a striking event marks a definite cleavage: the orgy scene.

In the chronological schedule underlying the plot, Curator Sauniere, Neveu's grandfather, is alive till the day the story begins. His murder actually sets the narrative machine in motion. Within Sophie' emotional world, however, his death dates back to years earlier, when an upsetting, actually highly traumatic event put a definitive end to Sophie's relationship to her grandfather.

Then, due to accidental circumstances, Sophie – unseen – had beheld his grandfather engaged in a mysterious and, to her, highly upsetting activity within an enigmatic sacred ritual. Sophie's experience is reported in chapter 32, but only in chapter 74, 168 pages being elapsed, information is shared about the actual sexual quality of the performance. With reference to the narrative structure, such long delay as well as the mysterious atmosphere surrounding the event gives Sophie's disclosure a cataclismatic character.

Sophie's exposure to grandparents' coitus is overwhelming: coitus is public and all the more traumatic inasmuch as reaching awareness unexpectedly. A dismaying experience of the primal scene characterizes then Sophie's relationship to parental dimension as much as to parents' definitive loss. In Sophie's relevant narrative material, sexual guilt and parents' death appear to be closely connected.

Two obvious qualities characterize the narrative treatment of the orgy scene: guilt and secrecy, *i.e.,* fear of being exposed and punished. Guilt clearly permeates the episode. Sophie's attitude after the events implies the most severe judgment towards grandfather. She assumes his guilt to be so extreme that she will never forgive him.

In the narrative manifest content, Sophie blames grandfather with a relatively uncommon sexual habit: public coitus. We have shown the main narrative included in *The Da Vinci Code* contains massive partial object level material and massive allusions to sexual union. I believe a comparison between the narratively manifest primal scene and concealed partial object level narrative may be very useful in order to fully understand the unconscious fantasy underlying Sophie Neveu's story.

The above reported detailed discussion of the main plot has brought to light abundant morphological analogies between objects and events in the narratives and the anatomy of the human body. Such analogies consistently configure the underlying unconscious fantasized intercourse as a male homosexual coitus. No reference to female body parts could be detected. Against such background, we believe we might get an easier access to the meaning of Sophie's traumatic experience if we come to think of it in terms of a homosexual intercourse.

We have stated above that two emotions pervade Sophie's response to the orgy scene: fear and guilt. She enters the family castle near Creully with caution. She goes silently down the secret stairs. The text details a state of real terror: "Heart racing", "She was frightened", "more eerie than the sound itself", "Heart pounding", "Holding her breath" (pp. 149-150).

We readers feel she is awaited by some unknown danger. The mysterious practice she is going to investigate is kept secret. Sophie fears she can be discovered. An exasperating fear to be exposed or punished dominate all the castle scene. At last she can see:

> The chanting grew steady again. Accelerating. Thundering now. Faster. The participants took a step inward and knelt. In that instant, Sophie could finally

see what they all were witnessing. Even as she staggered back in horror, she
felt the image searing itself into her memory forever (p. 151).

After Sophie is confronted with the orgy scene, her experience changes from
fear to anger and blame. Her judgment of grandfather's behaviours is immediate
and straightforward. The penalty is staggering: absolute and definitive rejection.
Grandfather's specific guilt is less clearly defined, yet.

However, reconstruction of partial object processes is once again
illuminating. Guilt. And actual social blame, are strongly associated in
postclassical European culture to homosexual behaviours. In fact, both secrecy
(*i.e.,* fear of being exposed to rejection and devaluation) and guilt issues may be
convenient to homosexual – anal penetrative, in the partial object material –
practices between men. In fact the novel main plot – which our analysis has
showed as including pervasive allusions to the male homosexual coitus – is
imbued with both fear and guilt feelings.

While discussing the main plot narrative and its underlying contents, we
have illustrated how exposure and sharing of intimate body areas is deemed to
elicit anxieties. Such anxieties included basic fears of been controlled, exploited,
invaded by the object's internal world, as well as the associate narcissistic fears
of perceiving the depth of our subjective needs for contact with and dependence
on powerful adults. The main plot, the struggle for the Cryptex, has told us a
story of vulnerability, of liability of both self-boundaries and self-image to
emotional injuries.

Sophie Neveu's family narrative, on the other hand, seems to include a
wider array of meaning. A partial object reading may well appear limiting and
one-sided. In Neveu's narrative, characters feature a meaningful personal
history. Sophie, specifically, is involved in an articulated web of relationships.

The painful account the author offers us of her life is dominated by the issue
of separation from parents. Sophies's mourning of their mysterious death, a loss
duplicated by her grandfather's murder, stirs our intense empathy, while the
final unexpected meeting with her two spared family members is able to ease
our readers' distress. We may identify with Sophie's feelings inasmuch as they
refer to the most basic and ubiquitous anxiety in infancy, separation anxiety
(Mahler et al., 1975).

Sophie's motives and anxieties definitely draw a complex network of
emotions and representations. This complexity and the most general parallel
with the structure of the human motivational system suggest we'd better
examine Sophie's parental narrative in terms of a (fictitional) individual's
interaction with her core love objects – to interpret Sophie's narrative also as a
sequence of interactions between *total objects*.

The manifest content of Sophie's narrative features a straightforward
temporal sequence: a) a blissful, unconflictual family atmosphere, as
exemplified by repeated affectionate and warm interactions with grandfather; b)
the sexual guilt; c) the traumatic and irretrievable cleavage of any relationship to

the Curator Saunier. This loss experience repeats and is implicitly equated with parent's and brother's sudden and mysterious death; d) the search for the *clef de vault;* e) the unexpected appearance of the surviving relatives with the reestablishment of an at length missed family experience.

In his comprehensive treaty on human dreaming activity, Freud has showed how dream formation processes lack communicational tools adequate to represent logical and particularly causal relations (1900, 315 ff.). In approaching the structure of Sophie's story, we cannot rely on surface causative chains.

Consistently, we will deliberately ignore this temporal sequence. We will put off any discussion of causal chains till we get a deeper understanding of the unconscious issues underlying the narrative. We will simply focus on the themes occurring one close to the other in the material.

Core sexual guilt in *The Da Vinci Code* lies in object choice. The choice of a sexually homologous, male sexual object. At a first level of observation homosexuality cleaves the bond to parental objects. And kill Sophie's brother, as obvious representative of male components of identity.

At this level of analysis it is irrelevant whether guilt is experienced by Sophie, rather than by Sauniere. From this point of view, I believe even the cognitive content associated with pain is irrelevant. Guilt, shame, disappointment are all implicit in the narrative. But the processes of displacement, condensation, projection, splitting, fragmentation of identity which characterizes dream thoughts (Freud, 1900, p. 283-344) make identification of culprit and victim extremely unreliable.

The reading of Sophie's narrative may on the other hand be deeply illuminated by the emotional and interpersonal background. We read of parental death, we read of excruciating feelings of loss and we read of homosexuality. In discussing *The Da Vinci Code* main narrative we have showed how a deep persecutory feeling is associated there with male homosexual themes. Sophie's narrative replicate the working through of unconscious experiences associated with male homosexual drives at a different level.

We have just stated substantial evidence suggests the narrative of Sophie's family warrants a total object reading. In this deeply moving, albeit secondary plot, we see a dramatic fantasy representation of the impact of homosexual interactions on core relations. Actually on the closest relations, relations to parents. And impact is hard.

In Freud's view, separation from mother is the prototypical source of pain, mental pain in humans (1926, pp. 203-204). Before the establishment of object constancy, *i.e.,* the persistent introjection of parental imagoes, separation from real parents, particularly from mother, is equated with mother's death and amounts to the infant's and small child's basic, primeval terror (Klein, 1935, p. 266). Under a total object perspective, fantasy material from Sophie's developmental story adds an if possible more ominous and frightening dimension to the subjective experience of homosexual relations.

Sophie's narrative, however, does not end with her breakdown with grandfather. The novel goes on. The life-threatening struggle with evil forces ends in Saint Paul's cathedral. From that moment on, the emotional hue changes. Helplessness, and the climate of pervasive threat and fear step back. The main characters may resume their search for the ultimate truth in a new, reassuring atmosphere, and the Grail is now at hand.

Sophie and Langdom reach Rosslyn Chapel. And from the hut on the chapel premises "The smell of bread wafted through the opened screened door" (p. 440). Grandmother appears, with all her sweetness, availability and warmth.

As the reader will be able to see from the Decoding Grid, Cheuvel includes partial object qualities referring to the male body, specifically to the male pubis. In a partial objet perspective the reunion of Sophie and Cheuvel eloquently allude to an integration, actually the integration of male identity: an array of unavoidable childlike, dependent, needy traits, blended with various doses of self-assurance, generativity, initiative. The weak, disguised, anxiety provoking self-representation meets in Rosslyn Chapel with the wished for, cherished, properly father-like male image.

However, Sophie's and granny's meeting may yield us even more fruitful associations at a total object level. The meeting at Rosslyn completes Sophie's story. Primal scene had torn relations to pieces. It had broken up irretrievably the trust between generations, between children or anyway dependent subjects and a core love object – a mother-like object. Now family is together again. The process of identity integration, of re-integrating components of male identity is associated in Sophie's narrative to the re-integration of family ties, to the rediscovery of the basic life dimension of interpersonal love.

Dawn

Alone,
In the dark.
A desperate,
Excruciating void
Around me.

It was night.
Now day has come,
And far away
A light blue beam shines.

Your kind smile,
Your love,
Your warm coils.

A piece is still missing from the puzzle, though. Where is mother? Where is maternal function represented in Sophie's story or in the novel as a whole. We will be looking for this final piece of evidence in the last section of the present chapter.

THE LONG SEARCH FOR THE GOOD MOTHER

The Institutional-Level Characters

The Da Vinci Code tells a story of individuals: a fascinating art scholar, a woman cryptologist, members of police, a professional historian, a killer, a bishop. But also the fictitious story of an institution: the Catholic Church.

In fact, individual characters move against the background of an epic struggle at an institutional group level: the Catholic Church, better an articulation of the latter, the supposedly all-powerful Opus Dei, versus an idealistic, generous, philanthropic community, the secret society Priory of Sion.

Opus Dei is a Catholic *prelatura personale* (Allen, 2005). It actually amounts to a Catholic religious movement, a free association among clergy and lay believers, which share intense religious experiences, including attendance to liturgy and meetings for common prayer and religious exploration.

Participation in a religious movement obviously implies the establishment of highly valued interpersonal relations, which tend to be stronger and deeper than social relationships among the general members of any geographically or politically defined community. This has a necessary impact also on various aspects of material life. To a minimum, participants in a religious movement are notoriously more likely to search for and establish financial or entrepreneurial partnerships (no less than marital ties) with fellow members than with people outside the boundaries of the community.

Opus Dei was founded by Mgr. Escrivá de Balaguer (1902-1975). Among Catholic organizations, it lends a unique value to participation in a working, productive life. This dimension, coupled with a customary secrecy with respect to membership, has sometimes attracted the attention of media and has made it a perfect choice to Dan Brown for an institutional character in his novel.

In *The Da Vinci Code*, Opus Dei is confronted by a formidable opponent: the Priory of Sion. To the Priory we cannot grant the same reality level as to the Opus Dei. Existence of the Priory has been reported to the general public only by a French occultist in 1956. Despite a biased but thorough investigation by

Baigent, Leigh, & Lincoln (1982) – actually a main source for Dan Brown's novel – factual evidence is substantially lacking.

In the novel the Priory of Sion is a secret – actually highly secret – society. Its fictitious features resemble in many ways the most famous secret societies of the past, including freemasonry and the mythical Rosecrucian society. The Priory would in turn represent an offspring of such institutions. Or better, most past, real and imaginary, secretive communities with interest in occult knowledge would amount to occasional surfacing of Priory activity.

The Confrontation

The struggle between the Catholic Church and the Priory makes up the basic overarching plot of the novel. All the events touching any individual character as well as all distinct secondary plots have their roots and find their ultimate meaning within this institutional framework.

We learn over the course of the novel that this struggle is an ancient one. Leigh Teabing's report (Chapter 54) dates it back soon after the Saviour's suffered and died on the Cross. At that early time, a group of Jesus Christ's disciples would have committed to defend and transfer from generation to another an ominous secret, supposedly very dangerous to the ecclesiastical organization.

The Church and the Priory would have been confronting each other ever since, the Priory defending and preserving the secret, and the Church trying hard to discover and destroy it forever. Dan Brown is particularly skilled in enrolling historical leaders as well as long-term strategies of the ecclesiastical institution in this battle for concealing the truth: we may mention the Roman emperor Constantinus the Great, the early selection of canonical books, the first Council of Nicaea, the damnation and slaughter of eminent members of the Knights of the Temple. On the other hand, distinguished intellectuals known for unconventional attitudes and particularly a dislike for the ecclesiastical organization are listed on the opposite side: Sandro Botticelli, Isaac Newton, Victor Hugo, Jean Cocteau – and above all the divine Leonardo.

The Matter at Stake

Only as late as in Chapter 60 do we come to learn the object of such an epical struggle and the unspeakable, ultimate secret – the quality and content of the mythical, eternally searched for Grail – is finally revealed to the readers. However, an uninterrupted flow of suggestions reaches us since the onset of the story, as the two adversary institutional forces come to be more and more characterised. Robert Langdon's competent lessons of iconology and above all Leigh Teabing's passionate harangue in Chateau Villette scene define clearly two semantic systems, we might say two confronting ideologies.

Experience of femininity is no doubt the core dimension around which such opposition appears to be organized. Femininity is described by Langdom in terms of a basic attitude, inscribed in all human realities. It would imply tolerance of individual and group choices, a basic option for nonviolent behaviours and social strategies, a joyful immersing into the bodily dimension of life, and particularly sexuality. In his *vis-à-vis* with severe captain Fache, Robert Langdon explains how pre-Christian (but pre-Greek would be a more accurate formula) religions allowed a definitely larger role to the feminine dimension, a core role which was reflected in the centrality of a feminine mother-like Goddess in Mediterranean pre-Doric religions. This sacred feminine has actually been the object of intense academic research and serious scholarship since the middle of XIX century, and still meets a keen interest within feminism oriented circles (Stone, 1976; Ruether, 2005).

In the fictive narrative, this very sacred feminine would be a source of enhanced concern to institutional Christianity, and particularly so to the Catholic Church. Langdom explains: "All I am saying is that Mr. Sauniere dedicated his life to studying the history of the goddess, and nothing has done more to erase that history than the Catholic Church" (Chapter 8).

Within this scenario the leadership of the Catholic Church would have been engaged since late antique, even early imperial time, to substantially alter Jesus Christ's teachings. While Jesus would have highly valued the sacred feminine, including the appreciation of an unregulated sexuality, the clergy, frightened by the possible social impact of this ethic of freedom, would have wasted enormous energies to the aim of concealing the feminine core of Christian kerygma.

In the novel we learn they would have faltered in front of no crime in order to maintain a feigned, male centred, sex intolerant, Christian ideology. To this aim, the Holy Scripture would have been altered, single individuals would have been murdered, wars would have been fighted. The main victims of such acts of violence would have been the members of the Priory of Sion.

In Langdom's and then Teabing's reports, Catholic community would display exasperated aversion to values associated with femininity. In *The Da Vinci Code,* evidence of such aversion is not offered, rather taken for granted. However, as we will show below, Dan Brown is here thriving on assumptions which are widely diffuse in contemporary western society.

The Grail

The Da Vinci Code is a narrative sprinkled with enigmas: all core information is encoded. Among the mysteries we come to meet over the narrative, one stands out as absolutely central: the mystery of the Holy Grail.

The Grail has been an enigmatic object for centuries. Despite some scholars arguing for different sources, Chrétien de Troyes drew the Grail imaginary from

Celtic mythology (Brown, 1910, Zambon, 2005). According to Loomis (1963, p. 58-60) the magic qualities of the Scared Grail can be traced back to some Celtic Gods' magic dishes or cups, ever dispensing food and wealth.

Chrétien grafted such wondrous, supernaturally gifted container into the European medieval literary environment. To this aim he couldn't help but embed it within an explicitly Christian background. Chrétien's death left his *Conte du Graal* in an unfinished state. And it so left forever unsettled the question as to the real nature of such a magic container. Interpretations multiplied both in medieval sequels of *Perceval*, as well as all through the following centuries. The Grail ultimate nature actually amounts to a major interest of European occultist of any denomination.

The Da Vinci Code is no exception. And the Grail enigma underlies the whole plot of the novel, posing the reader the basic questions: what is, ultimately, the Grail? What object or mystery the Priory of Sion *Senechaux* had guarded with their life? To these questions the novel actually gives three relevant answers:

a. The Grail amounts to the mortal remains of Saint Mary Magdalene.

b. To Magdalene's remains, we learn, a substantial collection of documents has been associated, giving evidence of both Jesus' free, open, feminine-oriented moral attitudes and of the information distortion practices consistently carried out by Church hierarchies, to the aim of concealing this very feminine values.

c. The Grail documents would in turn conceal an even more upsetting content, which would involve the most basic primal scene material in the novel.

Primal scene is the more traumatic the more it is unexpected. It aches the little child in as much as the parents' day behaviour conventionally exclude sexual activities among them. It aches the child inasmuch as he or she desperately clings to the believe that such daytime etiquette has a factual value, and extends to the realm of the night.

In fact, no more hurting a primal scene may we imagine than that involving Jesus our Lord. The Grail would concern this definitive, extreme primal scene experience: Jesus would have got married and Marie Magdalene would have borne a child to him.

The Institutional-Level Plot

The Priory and the Church would have been in perpetual conflict with each other. The novel offers us the narrative of a somewhat final and definitive struggle between the two institutional groups. Brown's writing strategies are here highly articulated. He is actually able to draw in front of the readers two highly structured but absolutely antithetic narratives reality. One reality is ominous. It is obviously upsetting to readers in any way sharing Christianity as their basic religious background. The other is reassuring, at least it is so to the same readership. We will refer to these narrative realities as a) the omen and b) the salvation.

A. THE OMEN

Within a) narrative series, the immense economical and political resources of the Catholic Church would be fully engaged to a single aim: concealing the content of the Grail mystery to humankind. In order to reach its aim the Church would hesitate in front of no crime: spying, stealing, lying, killing.

Various motives are offered for such a strategy. Basically they would amount to the clergy's wish to deprive humans of the sweetness offered by female values. These would obviously include the pleasures of sex as a basic component.

Envious of lay life and particularly of the freedom to engage in sexual activity it brings along, Churchmen would have felt the need to hide the joyful quality of sexuality, and to pollute the enormous potential for well being and meaning which contact with the feminine and the experience of childbearing can offer to human beings. A basic perquisite of such strategy would obviously be the ability to efface natural openness to sex purportedly displayed by Jesus, the very founder of the ecclesiastical organization.

The staggering, upsetting impact of such narrative phantasy on faithful readers cannot be overestimated. Features of such hostile representation of the clerical component of Christian community include envy, devaluation, control and frustration of human wishes. The extreme of mischievousness so alluded to can be fully grasped only against the background of the most obvious scriptural antecedent. In the Garden of Eden Satan speaks of God in the same colours as Professor Teabing's in his harangue against the Catholic Church:

ב וַתֹּאמֶר הָאִשָּׁה אֶל־הַנָּחָשׁ מִפְּרִי עֵץ־הַגָּן נֹאכֵל׃

ג וּמִפְּרִי הָעֵץ אֲשֶׁר בְּתוֹךְ־הַגָּן אָמַר אֱלֹהִים לֹא תֹאכְלוּ מִמֶּנּוּ וְלֹא תִגְּעוּ בּוֹ פֶּן־תְּמֻתוּן׃

ד וַיֹּאמֶר הַנָּחָשׁ אֶל־הָאִשָּׁה לֹא־מוֹת תְּמֻתוּן׃

ה כִּי יֹדֵעַ אֱלֹהִים כִּי בְּיוֹם אֲכָלְכֶם מִמֶּנּוּ וְנִפְקְחוּ עֵינֵיכֶם וִהְיִיתֶם כֵּאלֹהִים יֹדְעֵי טוֹב וָרָע׃

(Genesis 3, 2-5)

2 and the woman said to the serpent, "We may eat fruit from the trees in the garden,
3 but, from the tree that is in the middle of the garden – God said – You will not eat and you will not touch it, or you will die."
4 But the serpent said to the woman "You will not certainly die,
5 for God knows that the day you will eat from it your eyes will open up, and you will be like God, knowing good and evil."

In the biblical narrative Satan actually lied. And so did prof. Teabing in Dan Brown's novel.

B. THE SALVATION.

The Da Vinci Code plot features a definite and unexpected turnabout in the Saint Paul's Cathedral confrontation scene (Chapter 99 ff.). All of the various layers of the plot show here a discontinuity. At a partial object level, the threat of passive penetration is definitely loosened. In Sophie Neveu's family narrative, half of her family returns to life. At the institutional group level, the representation of the Catholic Church, or its powerful branch Opus Dei, is happily reversed. No more instigator of murders, no more international level corrupter of police officers, no more trainer of killers.

The revolution in the Church representation within the novel is summarised in the redemption of the character of Bishop Aringarosa. In the last pages of the novel Aringarosa, no more a hypocritical, ruthless conspirator, appears as an old man, being shot while desperately trying to save his misguided pupil Silas. Only then do we come to know he had been completely innocent of the Master's dismaying manoeuvres.

Church Identity

The Catholic Church has been addressed as *Ecclesia Mater*, Mother Church, since patristic (*e.g.* Tertullianus and Ciprianus in III century A.D.; cfr. Plumpe 1939) and maybe even apostolic times (Gal 4, 26). Institutions spontaneously gather parental features. In front of vast groups we unavoidable feel very small. And we direct to them our child-like, dependent wishes and needs. In fact, among basic social institutions, Church is the most mother-like. Through the explicit renounce to violence and to any virile power, the Church offers to her brethren the most appropriate institutional representation of motherhood.

Melanie Klein (1946, p. 4-6) taught us that the child as well as the childish parts of adult personality are prone to disarticulate mother's representation. Through the mechanism of *splitting* two opposing and highly polarized representations of mother are framed. The *good mother's* imago comes so to incorporate the cherished, beloved, highly idealized dimensions of the relationship with the caring mother. Such dimensions are so preserved from the ominous but unavoidable experience or memories of mother as angry, rejecting or however frustrating. The latter features are secluded in the *bad mother's* imago.

We are at last in the position to fully appreciate the shocking impact of the Da Vinci Code on a Church friendly readership, an impact which in turn is likely to have substantially contributed to its immense selling success. Probably no object representation is more vital to the human emotional well-being than the idealized good mother's. No wonder if in any culture a derogatory comment about mother is perceived as the most injuring insult. Contamination of the idealized mother's representation by negative qualities is bound to elicit immediate and severe emotional pain.

Under this perspective, the institutional narratives included in *The Da Vinci Code* poses a special burden to religiously committed readers, the more so to members of the Roman Catholic Church. Due to the unique, masterly swinging between historical and creative truth which characterise the style of the novel, the faithful reader is repeatedly threatened with the disintegration of the internal mother's representation.

A Short Note on Anticlericalism

Leigh Teabing's *cahier de doléances* against the Catholic Church is highly effective: it actually sounds convincing. For sketching such biased, malevolent representation of the Church, Dan Brown could thrive on a vast pre-existing literature.

We know too well church members have been the focus of surprisingly unmotivated blaming and consequent aggression all through history. Ethically austere Tacitus applauded Nero's decision to sentence many innocent Christians to an awful dead ("adfecit quesitissimis poenis", *Annales*, XV,44). He admitted they had no part in the arson of Rome, but he had no doubt they deserved to die all the same for their patent hate of the mankind ("odio humani generis", *ibidem*). Traianus (53-117 a.D.), the last great conqueror of Roman antiquity, showed some moderation against Jesus Christ's followers. He did not support active investigation on their activities, but never hesitated to deem the sole membership in the movement a capital offence. Although more learned adversaries of Christianity (e.g. Celsus, *Ἀληθὴς Λόγος*, or Porphyrius, *Κατὰ Χριστιανῶν*) rarely relied on such obvious slanders, Christians were widely blamed with cannibalism, infanticide and incest by the populace (Wagemakers, 2010). Third century persecutions are estimated to have wasted the lives of some thousand Christians (Frend 1984, p. 536-537).

We must avoid any possible personal distortion. Humans have perpetrated discrimination against many, maybe all forms of organized community religious life. Our memory aches in reviewing the long list of Hebrew pogroms, innumerable over the centuries, till the as yet last one, the great Nazi-operated Holocaust. Spanish *Reyes Catolicos* persecuted, expelled or killed thousands of Hebrew and Islamic subjects. Noble knights from the best German families didn't disregard killing and raping pagan peasants in the area bordering the state of the Teutonic Order.

Apparently, though very unluckily, human groups can find greater internal cohesion only directing devaluation and rage on minorities of any sort. The projective component of such attitude has been widely discussed and is well known to social psychologists (Gemmil, 1989) and anthropologists (Girard, 1972 & 1982).

However, in the present section we will definitely limit our discussion to hostility and devaluation directed to the Catholic Church. This institution and no other is the focus of the most awkward suspicions in the plot. We believe that the substantial role the Catholic Church and its implied misdeeds play in *The Da Vinci Code* are closely related to the basic unconscious structure underlying the narrative, and that this very major role was not inconsequential for the extraordinary commercial success of the novel.

From the point of view of the present discussion, two features of the Catholic institution are particularly meaningful. We have mentioned already the first one. The Church has a distinctive parental quality. Not only it is the focus of unlimited expectations for love and reliability, but actually parallels parents in offering moral guidance.

In social fantasy life, membership in a religious denomination implies a definite option with respect to parental ethical values. Every man is confronted with his or her parents' behavioural ideals and prescriptions. Sigmund Freud has shown how these ideals and prescriptions come to be introjected in the course of development and are incorporated in each individual's Super-Ego (1933, p. 70).

The vicissitudes of Super-Ego in adolescence and adulthood are obviously outside the scope of the present investigation. However, the believer makes an explicit option. He or she endorses the moral guidance his ancestors – including parents – have offered him. The Church – men's *mater et magistra* – defines a social space within which parents stay alive, cherished and obeyed all life through.

The Church parental imago, however, is not gender independent. We mentioned above how Church is *mother* to single believers. It is explicitly described as such in liturgical and pastoral texts. A major disagreement between the Catholic Church and other denominations has a specific relationships with sexual life: members of Catholic clergy are required to permanently renounce sexuality. As it is widely known, male clergy members detain an absolutely preponderant role within Churches, both in terms of institutional power and within the believers' fantasy life, as an identification between the priest and the person of Jesus Christ is implicitly and explicitly suggested.

By renouncing to sexuality the Catholic priest is somehow felt to partially renounce its full maleness. It's no incident that in modern societies priests were the only men required not to wear trousers, rather a cassock which bear similarities to a skirt.

In essence, widely shared representations of the Church and its members seem to allude to a couple imago: the implicitly omnipotent, everlasting mother church and her meek, caring, implicitly impotent, male attendants. We will now see how these imaginary couple representation contributes to eliciting particularly derogatory social fantasies. An adequate understanding of the latter will be of help to fully illuminate the Da Vinci Code institutional narrative.

Anticlerical Hate and Envy

Anticlerical hate has a specific focus: humans participating in a community life, sharing deep dimensions of their identity. To an external observer the faithful appears enveloped in the arms of a collective subject. He has renounced, or overcome adolescential fight against parental values. The faithful is inside: inside the church, implicitly inside the mother. Having chosen, maybe eagerly and instinctively, may be through the mastering of deep Oedipal conflicts, to dive in a collective subject, the believer establishes diffuse social love ties.

In fact, anticlerical hate has an Oedipal base. Envy of a love relationship, of a somewhat symbiotic, unambivalent relationship to the internal mother is a major motivational force supporting it. Within such constellation the Church imago comes to be a strategic and convenient target. Devaluating the Church imago – as Leigh Teabing's derogatory outline of Church history so effectively does – amounts to hurting a faithful's most intimate and cherished internal representation: the mother's imago.

Within traditional anticlerical propaganda clergy members are the focus of a no less vicious animosity than the institutional object. Priests were ruthlessly guillotined during the French Revolution, lost their lives in Stalin's icy Gulags, and were shot in thousands in various civil struggles the world over, from October Revolution to the Cristeros rebellion in Mexico, or the Spanish Civil War.

Sexual misconducts has been an unusually prevalent issue in the widely shared social aversion to church ministers, from the polemics on the "cura pederaste" in XIX century Spain (Vaquez Garcia, 2018) to the contemporary mediatic movement campaigning against instances of clerics-related sexual abuse.

Sexual life of clerics has been historically the focus of immoderate interest by the public. From Pietro Aretino's *Ragionamenti* to XIX and XX century Spain, it has been a basic dimension of pornographic literature, licentious drama and lubricous folk songs. Clerical sexual activities has been classified as implicitly predatory, violent and abusive. A wide literature has blamed the Catholic understanding of human sexuality as basically faulty. The imposition of generalised sexual taboos would made the average priest the helpless victim of uncontrolled and perverted drives (*cfr.* Keenan, 2011).

Relying on the works by Drewermann (1988), Mitchell (1998) writes: "Out of the knot of masturbation anxieties emerges sadism, masochism and every combination of the two; sexually addicted priests, priests with paraphilia, priests who rape, priest who sodomizes or arranged to be sodomized by altar boys" (p.

30 – 31). Within this view, the indiscriminate slaughter of clerics would amount to a sad but unavoidably consequence of the hypocritical clergy's sexual incontinence and of the resulting social outrage.

Literature on clerical sexual abuse shows a startling consistency with Leigh Teabing's ideology and is no doubt a basic source for Dan Brown's narrative. However, we must take note that sexual misconducts of some priests have been a main argument in anticlerical propaganda in most geographical and historical contexts. This suggests an unelaborated unconscious social phantasy is at play. Its content is very likely to feature prominent Oedipal themes.

Not only cannot Oedipal envy tolerate couple interactions between other individuals. It also clearly represents a major obstacle to the establishment of mature, couple relationships. Persisting enmeshment with internal and external parental objects hinders genuine separation processes and the full cathexis of age appropriate extrafamilial sexual partners. In fact, since the seminal works by Sigmund Freud, the overcoming of the Oedipal complex is deemed to be a perquisite for a proper access to latency and later on to the genital stage of libidinal development (Freud, 1924).

Within this framework, hate and devaluation of clergyman can serve specific psychological function. The priest has formally and symbolically renounced genitality. He is uniquely devoted to the maternal ecclesiastical institution. He is fully immerse in the community emotional life, in some way he lives and works at the very core of it, while not being willing to establish a marital couple life and serve any explicit parental function. The priest's life-choices happen to coincide with some specific aspects of unconscious fantasies underlying anticlerical ideology. To a community permeated by Oedipal anxieties this very features make him a highly convenient identificatory object.

Hate towards the priests undoubtedly includes projective components. It involves the projection of the unconscious shame and self-devaluation feelings associated with the Oedipal constellation: the inability to free himself from an inexhaustible jealousy for the possess of the mother and to fully confront women as an adult generative partner.

In essence, the inclusion in *The Da Vinci Code* of widespread contents of anticlerical propaganda seems to suggest main unconscious themes underlying the narrative include the following: a) a specific hate and envy for the blissful mother-child unconflictual symbiosis and b) projected feelings of shame and self-devaluation, stemming from the inability to confront an ominous father image and to fully meet mother's expectations.

Fear and Relief

Valuable advice

I turned to him in pain,
The Universe spinning around
The wrong way.
Bizarre lights,
Flashed
Where the sun had been shining
Just a second earlier.
The drake,
Enormous and shrewd,
Was definitely out to me.
Gestapo officers
Chattered
While planning
To experiment on my living flesh.
"There is no need to flee," –
The old man told me –
"Mother earth is still here,
Next to you, close, warm,
And loving".
I stared at the green hills,
At the rivers flowing by.
The meadows
Smiled and blinked
Under the mild Eastern wind.
My eyes got full
With gratitude and relief.

An adequate understanding of the fictitious struggle between the Church – or Opus Dei – and the Priory of Sion is now at hand. Data presented so far allow us to finally draw a meaningful picture. Mother – rather, mother's imago – is at stake.

In fact, mother's imago appears in two fully opposing states in the novel. We have a) a wicked, treacherous, lying mother, used to working stealthily and to manipulating children, *i.e.,* to controlling their behaviours through the systematic concealment of substantial amount of knowledge; and b) a life bearing, nurturing, caring, love object. A) imago is manifestly described in the novel, mainly in Leigh Teabing's views on the Catholic Church. The second imago lies for long outside of the manifest narrative, until resurfacing spontaneously, when the plot resolution lets loose of our idealized internal mother's representation.

Clergy's representation also undergoes a parallel cataclysmic shift through the novel. The alluded identification of Monsignor Aringarosa and the wicked Master endows the Prelate of the Opus Dei with a dark hue over a long segment of the story. We readers believe him to be associated with the albino killer's dreadful deeds. In the reader's experience Silas' anal-phallic, aggressive, murderous qualities are implicitly traced back to Aringarosa himself and stand out as an imminent threat for male bodily integrity.

Saint Paul's Cathedral scene changes everything. We rapidly learn Teabing's allegations against the church are factitious. The albino has been misled by Teabing's artful lies. The former's aims turn out to be unselfish. He has been moved only by the desperate love and concern for his ancient benefactor. Together with his Albino pupil Bishop Aringarosa loses all his phallic qualities. And turns into a weak, benevolent old man. No more powerful ominous father, he takes on a child role in the Oedipal competition, his penis being little and weak, as his name implies.

In the end, Mother is safe.

Chapter Six
To a Code, His Solution

MAPPING THE UNCONSCIOUS READING EXPERIENCE

By now, we have investigated several dimensions of Dan Brown's *The Da Vinci Code*. We have discovered a substantial amount of concealed contents and meanings. We may now turn the cogwheels: we may open the Criptex, unfold the full sequence of disguised emotional events and reveal, reconstruct the unconscious fantasy (better, fantasies) underlying the story. To the aim of greater clarity, we will list the main fantasy segments in turn.

A. MOTHER IS DEAD

The Grail coils bones. Bones of Magdalene, Jesus' son's mother. Mother's bones, actually. The deepest secret in *The Da Vinci Code* novel is mother's death. Magdalene's death is concrete, no doubt. Sophie Neveu's mother's death is narratively no less concrete: drowned in a river, killed by the enemies of the Priory.

Within the novel, Mother Church is apparently still on her feet. But ethically, symbolically, she is dead. It is dead as a source of hope, as a breast to turn to for care and support. The mother object's emotional death makes up the unconscious scenario underlying *The Da Vinci Code* plot.

The story does not lack a later resurrection. Before that, though, the full narrative sequence, need be consumed.

B. TRIANGULATION.

Mother's death is an obvious source of anxiety and fear. However, analysis of partial object narratives, particularly of Langdom-related subplot, suggests such anxieties and fears arise within a specific relational scenario. Data from partial object material point to male homosexual relations.

Mother withdraws, maybe rejects. Woman is far away, cold. Subject's desperation turns into blame. We have believed in women. We have believed in mother's genuine love. We now realize it has been just a lie. In fact, Mother Church is represented in the first section of the novel, as well as in common anticlerical propaganda, as distinctively deceiving men.

Such massive devaluation of the female love-object serves an obvious defensive function. It helps the subject to split and project his deep feeling of worthlessness. The experience of rejection and poor investment from mother is reversed and reprojected on a devaluated and wicked imago of hers.

The most immediate effect of this rejection of women is a narrowing distance from men: the idealization of father's imago – as so brilliantly exemplified by the noble, learned, unselfish character of Jacques Sauniere, the Louvre Curator. Closeness to father can effectively sooth anger to mother, sister, lover or wife. It can yield the love and appreciation so painfully missing from them. And can as well implement an effective retaliatory strategy. It exposes mother to feelings of jelousy and exclusion from a deeply tied and intimate couple.

That for the mother. But we will soon see that self experience is not as easy.

C. PARANOID FEARS

The Da Vinci Code is a novel of fear. The Master is always at work, blood-thirsty and ready to everything. Captain Bezu Fache is on the trail. Langdom is in constant danger of losing all, of being arrested, killed.

In our review of the novel main plot, we have widely shown that fears panging the main character, Langdom's fears, include abundant disguised allusions to male experience of passive penetration. Male is helpful. Relationship to father loosen mother's power and control. But exposes the subject, be it a boy or a regressing man, to the danger of an invasion/violation of intimacy: the somatic danger of an invasion of the inner body and the symbolic danger of an invasion of the deepest layers of the self.

At the same time, closeness to father seriously jeopardise Self representation. In front of father, of the phallic father, we are no more worthy of a place in adult society. Father-like wishes of control and power in the homosexual interaction inevitably push the male recipient backward along the developmental path. Submission, inferiority, inability to stand, feelings which have all been buried for a long time, together with childhood memories, resurface in the inner world.

Worst of all, the cherished unconscious fantasy of being a partner to mother – *i.e.,* socially and realistically to be a sexual partner of an adult female – cannot but crumble. Sadly, through triangulation the love object is all but regained. Rather, it withdraws further away. Homosexuality pushes the male in a highly precarious position. The more the subject comes close to the same sex partner, the more triangular pressure is exerted on the authentic, deep mother–like love object. But at the same time, the more the subject comes close to the same sex partner, the more adult identity is lost and the object rejection is magnified.

Homosexual seductive power is costly. The subject can gain it only through the resignation to others of the control of bodily boundaries: only at the cost of intense paranoid fears.

D. RELIEF

On closing my copy of *The Da Vinci Code,* having read it through to the last page, I felt deeply relieved. The main characters were safe. Sophie Noveu's family had turned out to be surprisingly alive. Aringarosa had been cleansed from horrific suspects. The Church had not been plotting in the dark to the aim of wickedly controlling and adulterating human culture. The Church imago was no more at stake. My fear about core mother identity had dispersed. *The Da Vinci Code* narrative had yielded inner world safeness in the end, unexpected and soothing.

Mother was back. And, with mother, male identity had been restored: the female passive component, Sophie, the glamorous male academic, Langdom, the long haired grandmother, and Sophie's brother were together again. Homosexual danger was undone forever.

Langdom could now reverently kneel in front of mother's sanctuary. Love, maternal love only can make the subject free from fear, jealousy, trickery and betrayal.

FIGHTING AGAINST A DEAD MOTHER

Out cast

Outcast,
In the darkness.
Fighting icy waves,
Strangers' voices haunting my ears.

A black, heavy knot inside me.
Biting.
Collapsing the weary arches
My poor soul is resting on.

And the thought of you,
Fading away:
Memories still sweet,
Vanishing echoes
Of your bright smiles.

The Da Vinci Code chronicles a struggle. Manifest content reports a struggle for the control of the Cryptex, a representative of phallus. The manifest content itself, however, warns us that at stake is something different, the Grail, alluding both plastically and in terms of narrative sequences to the female genital, to the eternal feminine (Azzone, in press).

The story has also a narrative starting point, a primary fact able to stir the complex narrative machine. The novel opens up with the death of Curator Sauniere. We are told, however, that the struggle about the possess of the Grail dates much earlier, since apostolic times, to be specific since Mary Magdalene's, reportedly Jesus' wife's, death.

In fact, death of mother amounts to the actual beginning of the narrative. Death of mother, *i.e.,* emotional death of the mother object: withdrawal, coldness, bitterness. How painful it is when the breast, that is maternal love and cares, disappears, dies. Mental pain can have many sources: aggression, frustration of wishes, an overwhelming competitor. *The Da Vinci Code* deals with a specific dimension of emotional pain: the one arising from withdrawal of love.

The French psychoanalyst André Green (1986, pp. 142 ff.) was first in reporting an emotionally dead mother is often buried at the very core of narcissistically injured patients' identity. He alluded to "an imago which has been constituted in the child's mind, following a maternal depression, brutally transforming a living objet, which was a source of vitality for the child, into a distant figure, toneless, practically inanimate" (p. 142). This experience would leave a basic "psychical hole" (p. 146) to be replaced with "recathexes which are the expression of destructiveness". This would in turn elicit depressive symptoms in the transference situation.

In a previous book we have reported how intense emotional pain located within the mother object may also be a core etiological factor in depressive disorders (Azzone, 2013). However, mother's death, mother's emotional death, can be met by multiple responses. The unconscious fantasy underlying *The Da Vinci Code* tells us of a more strategic option.

Mother may be confronted in the interpersonal field. Manipulation of interpersonal relations may offer a chance to shed into mother feelings of competition, jealousy and rejection, the very feelings concurrently tantalizing the Self.

The unconscious fantasy underlying *The Da Vinci Code* narrative involves multiple allusion to betrayal, particularly to the betrayal of mother through a preferential interaction with a phallic, possibly exciting male object. In fact, in Green's view (1986, p. 157) homosexual attachment to father or his representatives is believed to be a basic component of the dead mother complex.

Freud believed the social success of a literary creation was dependent on its ability to give imaginary life to universally shared wishful fantasies. The astonishing, widespread sale success of *The Da Vinci Code* allows us to assume the novel includes allusions to unconscious fantasies which are shared by most or even all contemporary readers. *The Da Vinci Code* tells us something very important to men living in our society.

We owe to Melanie Klein the full appreciation of the centrality of the object relationship to the breast. In early childhood the child is completely dependent on mother for both emotional and physical survival. This interpersonal framework substantially shapes the early development of the infant's inner world.

In Klein's terminology the paranoid-schizoid position indicates a constellation of wishes, fears and defences, better a constellation of unconscious fantasies where mother's representation is subject to intense splitting mechanisms. The infant's unconscious fantasy life is then characterised by rapid swings form an idealized, omnipotent, unceasingly caring and nourishing mother, to a rejecting, ruthless, invincible, hated and violently frightening mother. Within Kleinian perspective, paranoid-schizoid mechanisms and fantasies, and particularly intense splitting of parental imagos, are far from restricted to early childhood and may be observed at play in adult psychopathology and more generally in even short-term regressive emotional experiences through the entire course of life. In addition, regressive unconscious fantasies have been reported to characterize many widely shared cultural products, including religions, myths and political beliefs (*e.g.*, Grotstein 2004; Segal, 1987 & 1997; Kapur, 2008).

It is no wonder, then, that in Dan Brown's *The Da Vinci Code*, one of the most successful novel in XXI century, the relationship to an omnipotent and heavily splitted mother's imago amounts to the backbone of the overarching unconscious narrative framework. Lester Luborsky & Paul Crits-Cristoph (1990, Chs. 7 - 8) have shown empirically that in clinical and nonclinical settings unconscious narratives are pervaded by negative representations of the object. And in the novel we are here discussing, rejection, malicious omnipotent control, systematic reliance on falshood and deception are the most prominent features of Mother Church representation.

Within Kleinian understanding of the unconscious human mind, the emotional handling of ominous and aggressive components of mother's representation amounts to the basic and universal task of the unconscious thought processes from childhood to old age. However, the subject's strategies aiming at controlling mother-related anxieties and soothing painful emotions are multiple and multifaceted. Unconscious fantasies may be pervaded by projection, which allows the redirection of aggression on other, less vital libidinal objects; a grandiose self-image may help controlling helplessness and worthlessness feelings in front of mother; acting out may more immediately evacuate into other individuals or the society desperation and loneliness; aggression may be turned onto the self in terms of depressive symptoms.

Unconscious strategies and resources are highly differentiated. *The Da Vinci Code*, however, shows us a specific defensive strategy. The subject of the unconscious fantasy underlying the novel confronts mother's rejection through a definite triangular interpersonal manoeuvre. He is able to cast the mother – and the reader in a sense – in the very interpersonal position he had been experiencing in front of her. He rejects her and let her feel abandoned and lonely. In fact, in the phantasmatic triangular scenario, another partner, a male partner, is now preferred to her.

The specific emotion at issue here is jealousy. However, jealousy, expectedly induced in the mother, is not focused on a competitive equal. No conventional "other woman" upsets the subject's relationship to the love-object.

Oedipal triangulation is obviously altered here. More subtly, the subject of the fantasy takes over the very position the mother occupies in the Oedipal configuration. He acts as a direct competitor for the erotic power and control of the male object. In the resulting inversed Oedipal configuration he challenges mother in her own specific ability: the ability to seduce father.

May such interpersonal strategy be successful? May really competitive strivings with an all powerful love object prove able to bend her and bring her back to concern and care? My clinical experience, both in psychoanalytic settings and in the real life of psychiatric practice, particularly in the nosographical area of personality disorders, would suggest "no" as the most appropriate answer.

In the narrative sequence Dan Brown offers us in *The Da Vinci Code*, mother object comes back quite unexpectedly. No hues of disappointment, resentment or jealousy surfaces in the last scenes around Rosslyn Chapel, particularly in the words of grandmother Marie Chauvel. The reappearance of Mother's imago spells away any cloud. Easiness comes back. But according to mother's inscrutable, immutable, overarching schedule.

On the other hand, we know for a fact that the triangular strategy which pervades all main narratives in the novel is consistently associated with intense fear. All through the text the main character, the iconologist Robert Langdom, flees from ominous, dangerous phallic figures. In the confrontation with a woman, seductive interaction with a male third is dangerous. It involves the specific danger to lose maleness, to lose any source of attraction and pride in front of the female love-object.

In Dan Brown's novel we have met with specific interpersonal constellations and associated defences. We have met with specific and poorly functional solutions to the often discontinuous but universal experience of rejection from mother. Actually, whenever mother is dead, *i.e.,* withdrawn and severely depressed, spiteful tricks and hostile interpersonal manoeveurs can do nothing to restore her generous warmth.

Clinical experience consistently teaches us that the ability to emotionally nurture others is rooted in a deep feeling and state of well-being. Interpersonal blackmail may prove able to control behaviour, but it can never sooth inner pain. Rather, it may even contribute further to maternal distress and emotional dysfunction.

Very early in my psychiatric training I learned that no prescriptive measure can enhance the emotional performance of psychiatric patients' parents. Family therapists have long realised any advice to this aim is deemed to failure and believe they can overcome such difficulty by dictating family members just the opposite of the desired behaviour (Watzlavick et al., 1967).

In fact, mental pain can be alleviated only through genuine interhuman sharing. This depend on adequate emotional responsivity but relies no less on the availability of relevant knowledge and interpretative models. The psychoanalytic endeavour specifically aims to increase knowledge about mental pain, so providing the analyst with the best conditions for the understanding and sharing of the patient's suffering.

We don't get as far as to suggest parallel processes of emotional understanding and caring should be encouraged or can be implicitly operating within healthy functioning couples and mother-child dyads. But we must be aware that no measure of sophisticated interpersonal skills can replace these basic emotional functions. Actually *The Da Vinci Code* unconscius plot reports a failed attempt to manipulate and control a withdrawn and dejected interpersonal object.

THE DA VINCI CODE AND WOMEN

The Goddess

Bloodthirsty,
Omnipotent,
Shaker of the high trees,
Lady of the bone-cracking
Wild beasts.
Cold ice
And warm embrace,
Giver of love
And lender of the sacred waters of life.
Whichever side

Of your infinite beauty
You confer
To my unlimited admiration,
I will never renounce you,
Savage Kali.

Nowadays, the acknowledgement and fostering of women's rights are widely shared attitudes. They are somewhat specific components of contemporary culture. *The Da Vinci Code* is firmly embedded within such values and beliefs system. More specifically, its narrative is staged against a framework where feminine and male values are in harsh conflict on the global political and ideological scenario. From this point of view, *The Da Vinci Code* thrives on feministic culture. Tenderness, sensitivity, nonviolence, and creativity are specifically associated with the female experience of human reality. Male emotional, motivational and ethical world would be informed by opposing qualities: enhanced aggression, obsession with power and authority, intolerance for free creativity and bodily pleasures.

Within the novel fictional narrative, wicked male sadists would be at war with the disciples of Marie Magdalene, the leading representative of true femininity. However, the psychoanalytic investigation of unconscious fantasies underlying the manifest content has led us to a somewhat surprising conclusion. In the various layers of the text we could find no convincing evidence of devotion to the breast-object, rather disappointment with the mother-object, male homosexual constellations and hostile aggressive manoeuvres aiming at hurting and subjugating the female object.

Such polar opposition between manifest and concealed, conscious and unconscious contents left me startled. I imagine the reader also may share a feeling of surprise and puzzlement. On the manifest level the female goddess is celebrated: and in the unconscious narratives the woman appears as a dangerous, ominous, wicked and powerful liar. Members of the *Priory of Sion* have supposedly undergone a thousand years long painful and bloody fight in order to defend the secret of the sacred sexual union with the woman: and partial object content is distinctively and consistently devoid of representatives of the female body, at least until the final coup de théâtre allows Langdom to enter the sacred space of Rosslyn Chapel.

We have reported shortly above that *The Da Vinci Code* undoubtedly reflects widely shared views of role conflicts between the two sexes. Does the unconscious narrative underlying the text have something to tell us about contemporary social trends? Can our reading of the plot allow us to better understand the ostracism which has flooded male role and identity, since the twentieth century (Recalcati, 2011; Azzone, in press)?

Over the last couple of generations the father has been pitilessly put at the stake. His power has been criticised, then annihilated. He can rely no more on an implicit social solidarity for the interpersonal weakness and vulnerability which his relationship to the woman is bound to bring about. He enjoys no more the valued role as the sole responsible for the family income. He struggles with helplessness in front of adolescent sons' opposition and devaluation.

Social spread of narcissism and behaviours associated to oral dependency is sometimes understood in media and popular culture in terms of a collapse of father's authority. However the fault for such occurrences is laid again on adult men's frailty and lacking responsibility.

The reader should not fear I am here willing to blame anyone. Contemporary advocates of male resurgence are engaged in a childish and fated rebellion towards prevailing social trends. Rather, we need an exhaustive awareness of the complexity of heterosexual relationships and their implicit burden. Actually, couple life is rewarding, but as much emotionally expensive. A deep interaction with a woman cannot but drain many resources.

Handling female tumultuous emotionality may well prove an arduous task. Pregnancy, breast-feeding, the task of raising children, the trial of letting separation processes proceed in adolescence pose such heavy a burden on female shoulders. Closeness to a woman necessarily involves availability to share the full span of such emotional ordeal. It implies exposing oneself to rage, desperation, jealousy, and above all to emotional pain.

The unconscious narrative underlying *The Da Vinci Code* tells us of a possible outcome this emotional struggle can have: withdrawal from the woman. And envy, painful envy, focused on fellow male human beings, genuinely available to an however strenuous interaction with mothers, sisters, lovers, wives.

SOMETHING NEW AND SURPRISING

Before offering the reader our comprehensive interpretation of *The Da Vinci Code* we had formulated a number of principles which would have guided our application of the psychoanalytic theory and interpretative tools to the field of literary criticism. We have then suggested that a psychoanalytic reading of a literary text could be deemed valuable inasmuch as it could meet the following two perquisites: a) that the analysis could reveal unconscious contents which included wishes, fears, affects and relationship styles not apparent in the manifest narrative; and b) that the previously concealed material was suitable to suggest novel perspectives about the text, allowing it to be located differently within its historical, social, cultural, or literary framework. In essence we have proposed that a psychoanalytic reading of a literary text was valuable inasmuch as it could produce something new, some original cultural content which did not and could not exist without and outside this specific critical stance.

We hope the reader will agree the understanding of Dan Brown's *The Da Vinci Code* we have here proposed has largely met the two mentioned criteria. The novel manifest narrative claims devotion to and reliance on the female perspective: the unconscious narrative gives evidence of fear of and competition with women. The manifest narrative tells of the blissful sexual union with women: partial object material is consistently focused on male homosexual intercourse. Manifest content is filled with fear of male aggression: unconscious narratives are filled with fear of men's sexual appeal.

Reliance on psychoanalysis as an interpretative framework offered here a radically new narrative sequence. And this new reading allowed us in turn to develop novel insights in a number of social and psychological phenomena. We could detect in the text evidence of the most primal and universal human terror, fear of mother's death. We could better understand couple conflicts and the possible role triangular manoeuvres may play within them. In addition, we could formulate new hypothesis on the unconscious motives underlying anticlerical hate.

Under the psychoanalytical lens the text appeared under a new light. This is actually the most we could ask from it. Definitely, we are not even touching the question of truth, here. Reading is a subjective experience, better, a dyadic encounter. The most diverse emotional interactions may arise just as in any other relationship. We surely need not be advocate of postmodern criticism to admit any response to a text is subjectively justified, and subjectively highly valuable. And this is true also for the highly articulated and methodologically sophisticated responses to texts which goes by the name of literary criticism. We have only demonstrated here that psychoanalytically based criticism is a valuable, productive critical tool. We hope some readers will also agree and keep on exploiting its substantial investigative potential.

REFERENCES

Quotations from Dan Brown's *The Da Vinci Code* are drawn from the following edition:

Brown D. (2004) *The Da Vinci Code.* Special illustrated edition. Bantam Press, London-Toronto-Sydney-Auckland-Johannesburg.

Quotations from Sigmund Freud's works are drawn from the complete German edition:

Bibring E., Hoffer W., Kris E., & Isakower O. (eds.) (1940-1968) *Gesammelte Werke.* XVIII Banden. All translations are by the present author.

Afanasjev A.N. (1873) *Народные русские сказки.* 2nd ed., 3 vols. Tr. It. (1994) *Fiabe popolari russe.* Newton Compton, Roma.
Allen J.L. (2005) *Opus Dei: An Objective Look Behind the Myths and Reality of the Most Controversial Force in the Catholic Church.* Doubleday, New York.
Azzone P. (2010) Looking through a distorted mirror: Toward a psychodynamic understanding of descriptive psychopathology of depression. *The Journal of the American Academy of Psychoanalysis and Dynamic Psychiatry*, 38(4), pp. 575-605.
————. (2013) *Depression as a Psychoanalytic Problem.* University Press of America, Lanham, Md.
————. (2018) Matrix of the mind. An investigation into mother–child continuity. *International Journal of Applied Psychoanalytic Studies,* 15, pp. 29-42.
————. (in press) Sviluppo adolescenziale e misticismo nel *Conte du Graal.* In G.M. Ruggiero (ed.) *Psicoterapia e Mistica.*
Baigent M., Leigh R., Lincoln H. (1982) *The Holy Blood and the Holy Grail.* Johnatan Cape, London.
Baranger W. & Baranger M. (1961/1962) La situación analítica come campo dinámico. *Rivista Uruguaya de Psicoanálisis* 4(1). New ed. in (1969) *Problemas del campo psicoanalìtico*, pp. 129-164. Kargieman, Buenos Aires. It. ed. (1990) La situazione psicoanalitica come campo dinamico. In *La situazione psicoanalitica come campo bipersonale*, pp. 27-71. Raffaello Cortina Editore, Milano.
Barthes R. (1970) *S/Z.* Editions du Soleil, Paris.
Berman E. (1993) Introduction. In E. Berman (Ed.) *Essential Papers on Literature and Psychoanalysis*, pp. 1-18. New York University Press, New York & London.
Bion W.R. (1957) Differentiation of the psychotic from the non-psychotic personalities. *International Journal of Psychoanalysis*, 38(3-4), pp. 266-275.

————. (1961) *Experiences in Groups and Other Papers*. Tavistock, London.

————. (1962) *Learning from Experience*. William Heinemann Medical Books, London.

Bonaparte M. (1933) *Edgar Poe, Étude Psychanalytique*. Denoël et Steele, Paris.

Bonaparte M., Freud A., Kris E. (eds.) (1950) *Aus den Anfängen der Psychoanalyse 1887-1902. Briefe an Wilhelm Fliess, Abhandlungen und Notizen aus den Jahren 1887-1902*. Imago Publishing, London.

Brown A.C.L. (1910) The bleeding lance. *PMLA, 25*, pp. 1-59.

Celsus, Ἀληθὴς Λόγος, Mod. ed. and It. tr. by S. Rizzo (1989) *Contro i cristiani*. Rizzoli, Milano.

Chrétien de Troyes, *Le Chevalier au Lion*. Ed. and modern French transl. by D.F. Hult (1994) *Le Chevalier au Lion ou le Roman de Yvain*. Librairie Général Française, Paris.

————. *Le Chevalier de la Charrette*. Ed. by M. Roques (1983) Honoré Champion Editeur, Paris.

————. *Le Conte du Graal*. Ed. and modern French transl. by Ch. Méla (1990) *Le Conte du Graal ou le Roman de Perceval*. Librairie Général Française, Paris.

Cohen M. (2004) The Da Vinci Code dynamically de-coded. *Journal of the American Academy of Psychoanalysis and Dynamic Psychiatry*, 33(4), pp. 729-740.

Douglas M. (1966) *Purity and Danger: An Analysis of the Concepts of Pollution and Taboo*. Routledge and Kegan Paul, London.

Drewermann E. (1989) *Kleriker: Psychogramm eines Ideals*. Walter-Verlag, Olten-Freiburg im Breisgau.

Eifermann R.R. (1993) Interactions between textual analysis and related self-analysis. In E. Berman (Ed.) *Essential Papers on Literature and Psychoanalysis,* pp. 439-455. New York University Press, New York & London.

Fornari F. (1975) *Psychoanalysis of Nuclear War*. University of Indiana Press, Bloomington.

Frazer J.G. (1890) *The Golden Bough: A Study in Comparative Religion,* 2 Voll. Macmillan & Co., London.

Freedman B. (1987) Separation and fusion in *Twelfth Night*. In M. Charney & J. Reppen (eds.) *Psychoanalytic Approaches to Literature and Film,* pp. 96-119. Associated University Press, London – Toronto.

Frend W. H. C. (1984) *The Rise of Christianity*. Fortress Press, Philadelphia.

Freud S. (1895, edited with Joseph Breuer) *Studien über die Hysterie*. Verlag Franz Deuticke, Leipzig-Wien. Also in E. Bibring, W. Hoffer, E. Kris, & O. Isakower (eds.) (1952) *Gesammelte Werke*. I. Band, pp. 75 – 312. Imago Publishing, London.

————. (1900 – 8th ed. 1930) *Die Traumdeutung*. Verlag Franz Deutike, Leipzig & Wien. Also in E. Bibring, W. Hoffer, E. Kris, & O. Isakower (eds.) (1942) *Gesammelte Werke*. II-III. Band, pp. 1-642. Imago Publishing, London.

————. (1901) Zur Psychopathologie des Alltagslebens. *Monatsschrift für Psychiatrie und Neurologie*, X. Band, Heft 1 & 2. Also as E. Bibring, W. Hoffer, E. Kris, & O. Isakower (eds.) (1941) *Gesammelte Werke*. IV. Band. Imago Publishing, London.

————. (1905) *Drei Abhandlungen zur Sexualthoerie*. Verlag Franz Deuticke, Leipzig-Wien. Also in E. Bibring, W. Hoffer, E. Kris, & O. Isakower (eds.) (1942) *Gesammelte Werke*. V. Band, pp. 29-145. Imago Publishing, London.

————. (1905/06 - manuscript) Psychopatische Personen auf Bünen. In A. Richards (ed.) (1987) *Gesammelte Werke, Nachtragsband,* pp. 655- 661. Fischer Verlag, Frankfurt.

————. (1907) *Der Wahn und die Träume in W. Jensens Gradiva.* Hugo Heller & Co., Wien & Leipzig. Also in E. Bibring, W. Hoffer, E. Kris, & O. Isakower (eds.) (1941) *Gesammelte Werke.* VII. Band, pp. 31-125. Imago Publishing, London.

————. (1908a) Der Dichter und das Phantasieren. *Neue Revue. Halbmonatschrift für das öffentliche Leben,* 1, pp. 716–724. Also in E. Bibring, W. Hoffer, E. Kris, & O. Isakower (eds.) (1947) *Gesammelte Werke.* VII. Band, pp. 213-23. Imago Publishing, London

————. (1908b) Hysterische Phantasien und ihre Beziehung zur Bisexualität. *Zeitschrift für Sexualwissenschaft,* 1, pp. 27-34. Also in E. Bibring, W. Hoffer, E. Kris, & O. Isakower (eds.) (1941) *Gesammelte Werke.* VII. Band, pp. 189-199. Imago Publishing, London.

————. (1908c) Über infantilen Sexualtheorien. *Sexual-Probleme,* 4, pp. 763-779. Also in E. Bibring, W. Hoffer, E. Kris, & O. Isakower (eds.) (1941) *Gesammelte Werke.* VII. Band, pp. 171-188. Imago Publishing, London.

————. (1910) *Eine Kindeserinnerung des Leonardo da Vinci.* Schriften zur angewandten Seelenkunde. Heft VII. Verlag Franz Deuticke, Leipzig & Wien. Also in E. Bibring, W. Hoffer, E. Kris, & O. Isakower (eds.) (1943) *Gesammelte Werke.* VIII. Band, pp.127-211, Imago Publishing, London.

————. (1915) Mitteilung eines der psychoanalytischen Theorie wiedersprechendes Falles von Paranoia. *Internationale Zeitschrift für Ärztliche Psychoanalyse,* 3, pp. 321-329. Also in E. Bibring, W. Hoffer, E. Kris, & O. Isakower (eds.) (1946) *Gesammelte Werke.* X. Band, pp. 233-246. Imago Publishing, London.

————. (1916) Eine Beziehung zwischen einem Symbol und einem Symptom. *Internationale Zeitschrift für Ärztliche Psychoanalyse,* 4, p. 111. Also in E. Bibring, W. Hoffer, E. Kris, & O. Isakower (eds.) (1946) *Gesammelte Werke.* X. Band, pp. 394-395. Imago Publishing, London.

————. (1918) Aus der Geschichte einer infantilen Neurose. *Sammlung kleiner Schriften zur Neurosenlehre. IV. Folge.* Verlag Hugo Heller, Leipzig & Wien. Also in E. Bibring, W. Hoffer, E. Kris, & O. Isakower (eds.) (1940) *Gesammelte Werke.* XII. Band, pp. 9-57. Imago Publishing, London.

————. (1922, mauscript) Das Medusenhuapt. Published in E. Bibring, W. Hoffer, E. Kris, & O. Isakower (eds.) (1941) *Gesammelte Werke. XVII. Band,* pp. 45-48. Imago Publishing, London.

————. (1923) Die infantile Genitalorganisation. *Internationale Zeitschrift für Psychoanalyse,* 9(2), pp. 168-171. Also in E. Bibring, W. Hoffer, E. Kris, & O. Isakower (eds.) (1940) *Gesammelte Werke. XIII. Band,* pp. 291-298, Imago Publishing, London.

————. (1924) Der Untergang des Ödipuskomplexes. *Internationale Zeitschrift für Psychoanalyse,* 10, pp. 245-252. Also in E. Bibring, W. Hoffer, E. Kris, & O. Isakower (eds.) (1940) *Gesammelte Werke. XIII. Band,* pp. 393-402, Imago Publishing, London.

————. (1926) *Hemmung, Symptom und Angst.* Internationaler Psychoanalytischer Verlag, Leipzig-Wien-Zürich. Also in E. Bibring, W. Hoffer, E. Kris, O. Isakower (eds.) (1946) *Gesammelte Werke,* XIV. Band, pp. 111-205. Imago Publishing, London.

————. (1933) *Neu Folge der Vorlesungen zur Einführung in die Psychoanalyse.* International Psychoanalytische Verlag. Leipzig-Wien-Zürich. Also as E. Bibring, W. Hoffer, E. Kris, & O. Isakower (eds.) (1940) *Gesammelte Werke,* XV. Band. Imago Publishing, London.

Gemmil G. (1989) The dynamics of scapegoating in small groups. *Small Group Behavior,* 20(4), pp. 406-418.

Gill M. M. (1982) *Analysis of transference. Volume I: Theory and Technique.* International Universities Press, Madison, Ct.

Girard R. (1972) *La Violence et le Sacré.* Éditions Bernard Grasset, Paris.

————. (1982) *Le bouc émissaire.* Éditions Bernard Grasset, Paris.

Goethe W. (1774) *Die Leiden des jungen Werthers.* Weygand, Leipzig.

Green A. (1986) *On Private Madness.* The Hogarth Press, London.

Greenacre Ph. (1955) The mutual adventures of Jonathan Swift and Lemuel Gulliver: A study in patography. *The Psychoanalytic Quarterly,* 24, pp. 20-62.

Greenberg J.R., Mitchell S.A. (1983) *Object Relations in Psychoanalytic Theory.* Harvard University Press, Cambridge Ma.

Grimm J. & Grimm W. (1812-1815) *Kinder- und Haus-Märchen. Gesammelt durch die Brüder Grimm,* 2 Bände. Realschulbuchhandlung, Berlin.

Grotstein J.S. (2004) Spirituality, religion, politics, history, apocalypse and transcendence: An essay on a psychoanalytically and religiously forbidden subject. *International Journal of Applied Psychoanalytic Studies.* 1, pp 82-95.

Harpman J. (2011) *Écriture et Psychanalyse.* Mardaga, Wavre.

Hartman G. (1975) *The Fate of Reading and Other Essays.* University of Chicago Press, Chicago.

Holland N. (1968) *The Dynamics of Literary Response.* Oxford University Press, New York & London.

————. (1975) *Poems in Persons: An Introduction to the Psychoanalysis of Literature.* Norton Library, New York.

Issacs S. (1943) The nature and function of phantasy. In J. Riviere (ed.) *Developments in Psycho-Analysis,* Hogarth Press and the Institute of Psycho-Analysis, London. Also in P. King and R. Steiner (eds.) (1991) *The Freud-Klein Controversies 1941-1945,* pp. 264-321. Routledge, London.

Jackson L. (2014, 1st ed. 2000) *Literature, Psychoanalysis and the New Sciences of the Mind.* Longman, New York.

Jaques E. (1955) Social systems as a defense against persecutory and depressive anxiety. In M. Klein, P. Heimann, & R.E. Money-Kyrle (eds.) *New Directions in Psychoanalysis,* pp. 478–498.Tavistock, London.

Jensen W. (1903) *Gradiva. Ein pompejanisches Phantasiestück.* Reißner, Dresden & Leipzig.

Jones E. (1923) *Hamlet and Oedipus.* W.W. Norton & Co., London.

Kanzer M. (1950) The Oedipus trilogy. *Psychoanalytic Quarterly,* 19, pp. 561-573.

Kapur R. (2008) Kali: The Indian goddess of destruction and containing castration impulses in groups. *Group,* 32, pp. 35-43.

Keenan M. (2011) *Child Sexual Abuse and the Catholic Church: Gender, Power, and Organizational Culture.* Oxford University Press, Oxford.

Klein M. (1935) A contribution to the psychogenesis of manic-depressive states. *International Journal of Psycho-analysis,* 16, pp. 145-174. Also in (1975) *The Writings of Melanie Klein – Volume I: Love, Guilt and Reparation and Other Works 1921-1945*, pp. 262-289. The Free Press, New York.

———. (1945) The Oedipus Complex in the light of early anxieties. *International Journal of Psychoanalysis,* 26, pp. 11-33. Also in (1975) *The Writings of Melanie Klein – Volume I: Love, Guilt and Reparation and Other Works 1921-1945,* pp. 370-419. The Free Press, New York.

———. (1946) Notes on some schizoid mechanisms. *International Journal of Psychoanalysis,* 27, pp. 99-110. Also in (1975) *The Writings of Melanie Klein – Volume III: Envy and Gratitude and Other Works 1946-1963*, pp. 1-24. The Free Press, New York.

———. (1952) Some theoretical conclusions regarding the emotional life of the infant. In M. Klein, P. Heimann, S. Isaacs & J. Riviere (eds.) *Developments in Psychoanalysis*. Hogarth Press, London. Also in (1975) *The Writings of Melanie Klein – Volume III: Envy and Gratitude and Other Works 1946-1963*, pp. 61-93. The Free Press, New York.

Kris E. (1952) *Psychoanalytic Explorations in Art*. International Universities Press, New York.

Lacan J. (1966) *Ecrits*, pp 19-75. Edition du Soleil, Paris. *Eng. ed.* (1993) Seminar on the "The Purloined Letter". In E. Berman (Ed.) *Essential Papers on Literature and Psychoanalysis,* pp. 270-299. New York University Press, New York & London,.

Laplanche J. & Pontalis J.-B. (1967, 5th ed. 2007) *Vocabulaire de la psychanalyse*. PUF, Paris.

Leonardo da Vinci, *Codice Atlantico*. Edizione critica a cura di Augusto Marinoni (1975-1980) *Il Codice Atlantico della Biblioteca Ambrosiana di Milano*. Giunti-Barbera, Firenze.

Lewin B.D. (1933) The body as phallus. *Psychoanalytic Quarterly*, 2, pp. 24-47.

Loomis R.S. (1963) *The Grail from Celtic Myth to Christian Symbol*. University of Wales Press, Cardiff. Repr. (1991) Princeton University Press, Princeton.

Luborsky L. & Crits-Cristoph P. (1990) *Understanding Transference: The Core Conflictual Relationship Theme Method*. Basic Books, New York.

Mahler M.S., Pine F., Bergman A. (1975) *The Psychological Birth of the Human Infant: Symbiosis and Individuation*. Hutchkinson & Co., London.

Mauron Ch. (1950) *Introduction a la Psychanalayse de Mallarmé*. La Baconniére, Neuchâtel.

Meltzer D. (1973) *Sexual States of Mind*. Clunie Press, Perthshire.

Menzies I. (1970) *The Functioning of Social Systems as a Defense against Anxiety*. Tavistock Institution of Human Relations, London.

Milberg-Kaye R. (1987) Fanny and Alexander: A Kleinian Reading. In Charney M. & Reppen J. (eds.) *Psychoanalytic Approaches to Literature and Film*, pp. 180-191. Associated University Press, Cranbury, NJ-London-Missisauga, Ontario.

Miller M. (1956) *Nostalgia: A Psychoanalytic Study of Marcel Proust*. Houghton Mifflin Co., Boston.

Mitchell T. (1998) *Betrayal of the Innocents: Desire, Power and the Catholic Church in Spain*. University of Pennsylvania Press, Philadelphia.

Onorato R.J. (1971) *The Character of the Poet: Wordsworth in* The Prelude. Princeton University press, Princeton, N.J.

Otero, S. (1996) "Fearing our mothers": An overview of the psychoanalytic theories concerning the vagina dentata motif F547.1.1. *American Journal of Psychoanalysis,* 56, pp. 269–288.

Plumpe J.C. (1939) Ecclesia Mater. *Transactions and Proceedings of the American Philological Association,* 70, pp. 535-555.

Porphyrius, Κατὰ Χριστιανῶν. Mod. ed. with German and Italian translation by G. Musolino (2009) *Contro i Cristiani: Nella Raccolta di Adolf von Harnack con Tutti i Nuovi Frammenti in Appendice.* Bompiani, Milano.

Rank O. (1924) *Das Trauma der Geburt und seine Bedeutung für Psychoanalyse.* Internationaler Psychoanalytischer Verlag, Leipzig-Wien-Zürich.

Ransom J.C. (1941). *The New Criticism.* New Directions, New York.

Recalcati (2011) *Cosa Resta del Padre?: La Paternità nell'Epoca Ipermoderna.* Raffaello Cortina editore, Milano.

Ruether R.R. (2005) *Goddesses and the Divine Feminine: A Western Religious History.* University of California Press, Berkley & Los Angeles.

Seele A. (2000) *Frauen am Goethe. II ed.* Rowohlt Taschenbuch Verlag, Reinbeck am Hamburg.

Segal A. (1984) Joseph Conrad and the mid-life crisis. *International Review of Psychoanalysis,* 11, pp. 3-9.

Segal H. (1987) Silence is the real crime. *International Review of Psychoanalysis,* 14, pp. 3-12.

————. (1997) From Hiroshima to the Gulf War and after: socio-political expressions of ambivalence. In *Psychoanalysis, Literature and War: Papers 1972-1995,* pp. 157-168. Routledge & The Institute of Psycho-analysis, London

Skura M. A. (1981) *The Literary Use of the Psychoanalytic Process.* Yale University press, New Haven & London.

Spitz E.H. (1993) A critique of patography: Freud's original psychoanalytic approach to art. In E. Berman (ed.) *Essential Papers on Literature and Psychoanalysis,* pp. 238-261. New York University Press, New York & London.

Stone M. (1976) *Why God Was a Woman.* Barnes and Noble, New York.

Tacitus, *Annales.* Mod. ed. and It. tr. by C. Questa and B. Ceva (1981) *Annali.* Rizzoli editore, Milano.

Thomä H. & Kächele H. (1985) *Lehrbuch der psychoanalytischen Therapie, I. Grundlagen.* Springer Verlag, Berlin-Heidelberg. It. ed. by S. Freni (1990) *Trattato di terapia psicoanalitica. 1: Fondamenti teorici.* Bollati Boringhieri editore, Torino.

Tompkins J.P. (ed.) (1980) *Reader-Response Criticism: From Formalism to Post-structuralism.* John Hopkins University Press, Baltimora.

Vázquez-García F. (2008) La emergencia del «cura pederasta» y la batalla por la escuela en la España finisecular: El caso del escolapio Doroteo (Pamplona, 1899). *Recherches et Éducations,* 21, pp. 1-9.

Wagemakers B. (2010) Incest, infanticide, and cannibalism: Anti-Christians imputations in the Roman Empire. *Greece & Rome,* 57, pp. 337-354.

Watzlawick P., Helmick Beavin J., Jackson D.D. (1967) *Pragmatics of Human Communication; a Study of Interactional Patterns, Pathologies, and Paradoxes.* Norton, New York.

Werren D. (1993) Methodological problems in the psychoanalytic interpretation of literature: A review of studies on Sophocles' *Antigone*. In E. Berman (ed.) *Essential Papers on Literature and Psychoanalysis*, pp. 217-237. New York University Press, New York & London.

Zambon F. (2005) Introduzione. In Liborio M. (a cura di) *Il Graal: I Testi che Hanno Fondato la Leggenda*, pp. I-LXVII. Mondadori, Milano.